The Truth About Lies: How and Why We Deceive Ourselves and Others.

By

R.ANANDA RAJU

Introduction

In the labyrinth of the human mind, where truth and deception intertwine, lies cast their shadow, distorting our perceptions and veiling our realities. Welcome to "The Truth About Lies: How and Why We Deceive Ourselves and Others," a profound and enlightening journey into the intricate tapestry of human behaviour. Within the pages of this book, we embark on a quest to unravel the enigma of self-deception, exploring its profound implications on our lives, relationships, and the very essence of our being.

Deep within the recesses of our consciousness, we all have experienced the subtle dance of self-deception. It is a psychological survival tactic, a veil woven to shield us from uncomfortable truths or painful emotions. And yet, it is a delicate dance we often engage in unconsciously. But why do we resort to self-deception? What drives us to convince ourselves of falsehoods, to believe in illusions that crumble upon closer inspection?

"The Truth About Lies" delves into the fascinating science behind self-deception, unearthing its evolutionary origins that have intertwined with our very existence. From our earliest ancestors to modern-day humans, lying has shaped our species, providing us with adaptive advantages in the intricate tapestry of survival. Within these pages, we unlock the secrets of our deceptive nature, unravelling the threads that bind us to this timeless behaviour.

To navigate the labyrinth of deception, we must grasp the intricate psychological mechanisms and strategies we employ to deceive ourselves and others. The human mind, a vast landscape of thoughts and emotions, is both our greatest ally and our most cunning adversary. Through captivating insights and revelatory research, this book exposes the intricate interplay between truth and deception, illuminating the complex layers of our conscious and unconscious minds.

Yet, the consequences of self-deception are not confined to the isolated chambers of our psyche. They reverberate through the tapestry of our lives, impacting our mental and physical well-being, and the relationships we hold dear. "The Truth About Lies" navigates the treacherous waters of deception's aftermath, unveiling the profound effects of dishonesty on our individual and collective existence. As we confront these repercussions head-on, we are empowered to chart a course towards authenticity and self-actualization.

Ethics and morality stand as steadfast sentinels at the crossroads of truth and deception. They compel us to question the implications of lying and self-deception, challenging our beliefs and values. In this book, we confront the ethical quandaries that lie within the shadows of deceit, exploring the moral dimensions that shape our choices and actions. By engaging in this dialogue, we shed light on the intricate tapestry of truth-telling, forging a path towards a more compassionate and ethically grounded society.

Armed with knowledge and introspection, we embark on a transformative journey of self-discovery. "The Truth About Lies" equips us with the tools to recognize and overcome our own self-deception, guiding us towards a path of authenticity and personal growth. Moreover, it offers compassionate insights into navigating the lies of others, fostering constructive dialogue and understanding in the face of deception.

Drawing upon the latest research from psychology, neuroscience, sociology, and biology, "The Truth About Lies" weaves together a rich tapestry of scientific knowledge, real-life examples, and captivating stories. It transcends the boundaries of academia, inviting anyone who seeks a deeper understanding of themselves, their behaviours, and their interactions with others.

As you embark on this profound journey through the pages that follow, be prepared to confront your own illusions, challenge your assumptions, and embrace the liberating power of truth. Are you ready to uncover "The Truth About Lies" and step into a world of self-awareness and authenticity?

to uncover "The Truth About Lies" and step into a world of self-awareness and authenticity?

R.Ananda Raju

Ah, the enigmatic nature of lying and its evolutionary origins! In our quest to understand why we lie, we must delve into the depths of human psychology and the intricacies of our evolutionary heritage. Join me, dear reader, as we explore the evolutionary roots of dishonesty, peering through the lens of adaptation and survival.

At first glance, one might assume that honesty would be the prevailing trait in human interactions. After all, trust and cooperation are essential for the cohesion and functioning of social groups. However, the reality is far more complex. Lying, dear reader has woven itself into the very fabric of our existence, bearing the imprints of our evolutionary history.

To comprehend why we lie, we must journey back in time to our early ancestors. Our primitive predecessors lived in a world rife with competition, where survival depended on acquiring resources, mates, and protection. In such an environment, the ability to deceive conferred distinct advantages. Picture a hunter-gatherer seeking to secure a larger share of the spoils or a potential mate embellishing their qualities to enhance their chances of reproductive success. These acts of deception, rooted in the pursuit of personal gain, provided an evolutionary advantage, enabling individuals to navigate the complex web of social interactions and improve their chances of survival.

As our species evolved, so too did the complexity of our social structures. Our ancestors formed intricate social hierarchies, where the acquisition and maintenance of status held profound implications for survival. In such a context, lies became tools of manipulation, allowing individuals to rise in the ranks, gain resources, and secure reproductive opportunities. Deception became a strategic manoeuvre, employed to outwit rivals, gain allies, and solidify one's position within the social group.

Furthermore, the human mind developed remarkable cognitive abilities, including theory of mind—the capacity to understand and attribute mental states to others. This cognitive prowess opened the door to sophisticated forms of deception. We learned to recognize and exploit the vulnerabilities and expectations of our fellow humans, utilizing lies to manipulate their perceptions and shape their behaviours. From white lies to complex webs of deceit, our capacity for deception expanded, entwining itself with our social fabric.

But, dear reader, the evolutionary roots of dishonesty is not solely confined to selfish motivations. Altruistic lies, driven by empathy and the desire to protect others, also find their place in the tapestry of deception. Picture a mother soothing her child with a comforting falsehood or a friend offering words of encouragement to bolster the spirits of a loved one. These acts of deception, though not driven by personal gain, serve as social glue, fostering cohesion and maintaining relationships in the intricate web of human connections.

However, it is essential to recognize that while lying may have conferred adaptive advantages in our evolutionary past, it does not absolve us of the moral implications and ethical dilemmas it presents in the present day. Our evolved capacity for deception exists within a complex social landscape, where honesty and trust remain crucial for the functioning of modern societies. Balancing the evolutionary remnants of deception with the moral imperatives of truth and integrity is a delicate dance that challenges us on both individual and collective levels.

Dear reader, the evolutionary roots of dishonesty offer us a glimpse into the intricate interplay between our biological heritage and the ethical dilemmas we face in contemporary society. While lying may have served our ancestors well in their quest for survival and reproductive success, it is incumbent upon us to reflect on the moral dimensions of deception and navigate the complexities of truth and trust in the modern world. Only through introspection, empathy, and a commitment to ethical conduct can we transcend our evolutionary origins and foster a culture of honesty and authenticity.

Chapter 1

Once upon a time in the bustling city of Mumbai, there lived a young and inquisitive man named Arjun. His mind was a whirlwind of questions, and his insatiable curiosity drove him to seek answers to life's mysteries. However, it was the enigmatic nature of lies that captivated his imagination—the intricate dance between truth and falsehood that shaped destinies, mended hearts, and unravelled the fabric of reality itself.

Arjun, armed with a thirst for knowledge, embarked on a quest to unravel the complexities of human deception. He became a seeker of truth in a world veiled by lies, determined to navigate the labyrinth of deceit that permeated every corner of human communication.

With every step, Arjun found himself encountering individuals from diverse walks of life, each holding their own stories and experiences with deception. From humble street vendors to influential businessmen, he listened intently to their tales, extracting fragments of wisdom from the tapestry of their lives.

As he delved deeper into his journey, Arjun's understanding of lies evolved. He realized that defining a lie was not a simple task. Lies were not confined to outright fabrications; they encompassed omissions, half-truths, and even the intricacies of self-deception. The line between truth and falsehood blurred, revealing a complex and nuanced terrain that demanded careful examination.

Determined to make sense of this intricate web, Arjun sought to classify the multitude of lies that populated their human landscape. He began with the realm of white lies—the seemingly harmless untruths people told to protect others' feelings or maintain social harmony. With each encounter, Arjun recognized the delicate balance between honesty and compassion that drove these lies, understanding their role as social lubricants in the intricate fabric of human interactions.

However, as Arjun ventured further, he encountered lies of omission—instances where truth was concealed or information purposefully withheld. His conscience wrestled with the ethical implications of these lies, questioning when silence became a form of deceit and pondering the power dynamics that influenced our choices in divulging or concealing the truth.

Arjun's exploration led him to lies driven by personal gain, where individuals manipulated facts to achieve their own objectives. He witnessed the embellishment of qualifications, the fabrication of accomplishments, and the deceitful practices employed for personal advancement. These lies unveiled the darker shades of deception, exposing the potential harm they could inflict on unsuspecting victims.

As Arjun delved deeper into the labyrinth, he encountered lies told to protect others—a realm where individuals resorted to deception out of a sense of love, care, or perceived necessity. These lies posed profound moral questions, blurring the boundaries of honesty and challenging the delicate balance between truthfulness and the well-being of those we hold dear.

Yet, even darker truths awaited Arjun. He stumbled upon lies driven by malice—deception as a weapon to harm, manipulates, or gain power over others. The psychology behind such deceitful practices fascinated him, as he peeled back the layers of the human psyche to understand the motivations and consequences that fuelled these actions.

As Arjun classified and categorized the lies he encountered, he realized that they were not isolated incidents. They were intricate manifestations of human psychology, culture, and individual experiences. Lies reflected the desires for social cohesion, personal advancement, protection, and even the darker aspects of human nature. Each lie carried its own weight, intricately woven into the fabric of their lives, shaping relationships and influencing their understanding of truth.

Just as Arjun believed he had unravelled the vast landscape of lies, an unexpected twist awaited him. Amidst his exploration, a revelation emerged—a new type of lie that defied conventional wisdom and challenged everything he thought he knew about deception. A lie that he himself had told.

A lie is an assertion that is believed to be false, typically used with the purpose of deceiving or misleading someone. The practice of communicating lies is called lying. A person who communicates a lie may be termed a liar. Lies can be interpreted as deliberately false statements or misleading statements.

There are different types of lies, depending on their intention, their content, or their personality. Some lies are malicious, or meant to harm others, while some are jocose, or meant to amuse others. Some lies are of commission, or stating something false, while some are of omission, or leaving out something true, and some are of influence, or affecting someone's character. Some liars are compulsive, or lying habitually, while some are pathological, or lying without reason, and some are sociopathic, or lying without remorse.

Some examples of different types of lies are:

- White lies: These are lies that are told to protect someone's feelings or maintain social harmony. They are usually harmless and often expected in certain situations. For example, telling someone they look good when they don't, or saying you enjoyed a meal when you didn't.

- Blue lies: These are lies that are told for the collective good or in the name of the collective. They are often used by groups to justify their actions or beliefs, or to gain support or loyalty from others. For example, telling a lie to protect your team, your country, or your religion.

- Black lies: These are lies that are told for simple and callous selfishness. They are usually told when others gain nothing, and the sole purpose is either to get oneself out of trouble or to gain something one desires. For example, lying about your qualifications, your achievements, or your whereabouts.

- Gray lies: These are lies that fall somewhere between white and black lies. They are not entirely harmless or entirely selfish. They may be told for mixed motives, such as compassion, guilt, fear, or convenience. For example, lying to spare someone's feelings, to avoid confrontation, to keep a promise, or to cover up a mistake.

A poem about lying.

Lying

Lying is a game of words

A twisted dance of truth and lies

A skilful art of hiding and revealing

A subtle craft of shaping and deceiving

Lying is a tool of power

A weapon to harm or protect

A strategy to win or lose

A tactic to influence or manipulate

Lying is a test of character

A challenge to our morals and values

A choice to be honest or dishonest

A consequence to face or avoid

Lying is a part of life

A reality we can't deny

A dilemma we must confront

A lesson we must learn

Chapter 2

Once upon a time in a quaint town nestled by the countryside, there lived a curious and imaginative young girl named Maya. With her sparkling eyes and a mind brimming with wonder, Maya embarked on a captivating journey through the intricate landscape of childhood development.

As a toddler, Maya revelled in her vibrant imagination, conjuring vivid tales of magical creatures and fantastical adventures. Her parents watched in awe as she weaved intricate narratives, blurring the line between reality and make-believe. Little did they know that Maya's early foray into storytelling would sow the seeds of a remarkable journey.

As Maya grew older, her imagination remained as vibrant as ever, but her stories began to take on a new twist. It was during one sunny afternoon, while playing in the backyard with her friends, that she spun a tale about a hidden treasure buried beneath an ancient oak tree. Her friends, eyes wide with anticipation, followed her lead, ready to embark on a quest to find the mythical treasure.

Maya's ability to bend the truth fascinated her friends and intrigued her parents. They marvelled at her creativity, but they also noticed a glimmer of something else—a hint of mischief and an inkling of deception. It was at this moment that Maya's journey through the complexities of lying and truth began.

As Maya continued to grow, her desire for autonomy and avoidance of punishment played a role in shaping her relationship with the truth. She discovered that sometimes, a small fib could shield her from the consequences she feared. It started innocently enough, with a claim of finishing her vegetables when she had secretly fed them to the family dog. Maya realized that her parents, concerned for her health, were more likely to reward her if they believed she had dutifully consumed her greens.

But as Maya delved deeper into the labyrinth of deception, she encountered a crossroads. Her best friend, Rohan, had accidentally broken a prized possession belonging to their school. Fearful of the repercussions, Rohan turned to Maya, pleading for help. Maya grappled with her sense of loyalty, torn between her friendship and the weight of honesty. In that pivotal moment, she made a choice—the choice to protect her friend, to shield him from blame. It was a lie born out of love and a desire to preserve their bond.

As Maya navigated the social landscape of school, she witnessed the power of lies in shaping perceptions and gaining acceptance. Her classmates would often boast of their grand adventures or exaggerated accomplishments, weaving tales to garner attention and admiration. Maya found herself caught in a web of embellishment, sharing her own stories of extraordinary feats to fit in. She realized that lies could be a currency in the realm of popularity—a means to create an illusion of grandeur and secure a place among her peers.

But the more Maya delved into the world of deception, the more she grappled with its implications. A gnawing feeling tugged at her conscience, urging her to examine the consequences of her actions. With each lie, she sensed a crack forming in the trust she held dear. Maya longed for the authenticity that had once defined her, yearning to reconcile her desire for acceptance with the value of honesty.

It was during a school project on empathy and understanding that Maya's journey took an unexpected turn. As she researched and interviewed others, she began to unravel the complexities of human relationships and the fragility of trust. Maya listened to stories of betrayal, heartache, and shattered bonds—all stemming from lies woven with ill intent. The weight of these revelations bore down upon her, reshaping her understanding of deception.

In the quiet solitude of her room, Maya contemplated the profound impact of lies on the tapestry of human connection. She realized that the path she had embarked upon, one paved with half-truths and embellishments, was not the road she wished to travel. Determined to find her way back to the truth, Maya vowed to navigate the complexities of honesty with newfound integrity.

And so, Maya embarked on a transformative journey—one of self-discovery, introspection, and personal growth. She sought to redefine her relationship with truth, to mend the cracks in the trust she held dear. Maya learned that the path to authenticity and genuine connections required vulnerability, empathy, and a willingness to embrace the complexities of human nature.

As Maya continued on her journey, she discovered that the greatest treasures lie not in mythical troves but within the depths of her own heart. Through honesty and understanding, she unearthed the power to shape her own destiny, mend fractured bonds, and rewrite the narrative of her life.

And so, dear reader, as Maya's story intertwines with your own, remember the lessons she learned. Embrace the beauty of truth, cherish the bonds built on authenticity, and navigate the intricacies of lying with wisdom and compassion. For in the dance between honesty and deceit, lies the essence of what it means to be human.

Lying is a fascinating aspect of child development that emerges as children navigate the complex world of social interactions and personal autonomy. While it may raise concerns for parents and caregivers, it is important to understand that lying is a normal part of cognitive and social development. Let's explore how and when lying emerges in the developmental journey of children.

Early Childhood: The Seeds of Imagination

In the early years of childhood, typically between the ages of 2 and 4, children begin to engage in imaginative play. This newfound ability to create fictional scenarios and pretend enables them to experiment with storytelling and role-playing. During this stage, children may blur the line between reality and imagination, sometimes telling stories that deviate from the truth. While these narratives may not be outright lies in the traditional sense, they lay the groundwork for the emergence of more deliberate deception later on.

The Emergence of Self-Awareness

Around the age of 4 to 6, children develop a deeper understanding of their own thoughts, feelings, and desires. They begin to differentiate between their internal experiences and those of others, leading to a growing awareness of themselves as separate individuals. This newfound self-awareness paves the way for the emergence of lying as children realize that their thoughts and intentions can be concealed or manipulated through deception.

Desire for Autonomy and Avoidance of Punishment

As children continue to grow, they develop a sense of autonomy and a desire for independence. They start to recognize that their actions have consequences, both positive and negative. Lying may become a strategy to avoid punishment or negative outcomes. Children may fib about completing chores, finishing homework, or engaging in mischievous behaviour to protect themselves from reprimands or consequences they perceive as undesirable.

Social Influences and Peer Interactions

The influence of social interactions and peer relationships cannot be overlooked in the development of lying. As children engage with their peers, they begin to understand the power of deception as a means to shape perceptions, gain social acceptance, or avoid social disapproval. They may tell exaggerated stories or fabricate experiences to impress others, fit in with their peers, or gain attention.

Theory of Mind and Perspective Taking

Around the age of 6 to 8, children develop a more advanced understanding of the concept of "theory of mind." This refers to their ability to understand that others have thoughts, beliefs, and perspectives that may differ from their own. This cognitive milestone enables children to engage in more sophisticated forms of lying, as they become adept at considering the beliefs and expectations of others and tailoring their lies accordingly.

Cognitive Flexibility and Problem-Solving

As children progress through middle childhood and into adolescence, their cognitive abilities continue to develop. They become more skilled at thinking abstractly, problem-solving, and weighing the consequences of their actions. Lying may be employed as a strategic tool to navigate social situations, negotiate conflicts, or achieve personal goals. It becomes a reflection of their growing understanding of social dynamics and the complex interplay between honesty, deception, and personal gain.

It is important to note that while lying is a normal part of development, it is essential for parents and caregivers to provide guidance and support in fostering honesty and ethical behaviour. Teaching children about the value of honesty, trust, and empathy helps them navigate the complexities of truth and falsehood. By modelling integrity, open communication, and understanding, adults can contribute to the development of responsible and truthful individuals.

Chapter 3

Arjun was an enigmatic figure, his piercing eyes revealing a mind that delved into the depths of human psychology. With a penchant for unravelling the mysteries of the human psyche, he embarked on a thrilling journey to understand the psychological, social, and evolutionary reasons behind lying.

Arjun's quest began with a series of mysterious events. A renowned psychologist named Dr. Singh approached him with an offer he couldn't refuse. Dr. Singh, a mastermind in the realm of human behaviour, had discovered a hidden secret—an ancient artifact rumoured to possess the power to reveal the truth behind every lie.

Intrigued and fuelled by curiosity, Arjun joined Dr. Singh on a daring expedition to uncover this artifact. Their journey took them to remote corners of the world, where they encountered treacherous terrains, unyielding challenges, and clandestine encounters.

As they delved deeper into the quest, Arjun understands of lying expanded. Driven by psychological reasons, he learned how lies were often born out of fear, insecurity, and the desire for self-preservation. Arjun's own past experiences began to resurface, revealing how lies had shaped his relationships and influenced his own sense of identity.

The social reasons behind lying intrigued Arjun as well. He witnessed how lies could serve as the glue that held societies together, preserving harmony and avoiding conflicts. However, he also witnessed the dark side of lying, where reputations were tarnished, trust was shattered, and lives were shattered.

With each step of their journey, Arjun and Dr. Singh encountered individuals whose lives had been deeply impacted by lies. They met a young woman whose entire existence had been built on a web of deceit, forced to assume different identities to escape a haunting past. They crossed paths with a charismatic leader who used lies as a means to manipulate and control those around him. The stories they encountered were gripping, filled with suspense and unexpected twists.

As their adventure neared its climax, Arjun and Dr. Singh discovered a hidden lair—a chamber buried deep within an ancient temple. There, they found the coveted artifact, a shimmering gem that pulsated with an otherworldly energy.

Little did they know that they were not alone. A shadowy figure, driven by his own insidious motives, had been following their every move. Viren, a master of deception, craved the power of the artifact for his nefarious schemes.

A thrilling chase ensued as Arjun and Dr. Singh raced against time to unlock the truth hidden within the gem. Viren, relentless in his pursuit, unleashed a torrent of lies, illusions, and mind games to thwart their progress. The lines between reality and falsehood blurred as they traversed through a labyrinth of deceit.

In a climactic twist, Arjun uncovered a shocking revelation—the artifact itself was a manifestation of lies. It possessed no power to reveal the truth, but rather amplified the lies that surrounded it. It was a metaphorical mirror, reflecting the darkness and complexity of the human condition.

Armed with this newfound understanding, Arjun realized that the quest for the truth lay not in an external artifact but within the depths of human introspection. The true power to unravel the mysteries of lying resided in self-awareness, empathy, and a commitment to authentic communication.

In a final showdown, Arjun confronted Viren, their battle raging on both physical and psychological fronts. Drawing upon his knowledge of the psychological, social, and evolutionary reasons behind lying, Arjun outwitted Viren's manipulations and exposed his deceitful schemes.

In the aftermath, Arjun returned home, forever changed by his journey. Armed with wisdom and empathy, he dedicated himself to helping others navigate the complexities of lying and the profound impact it had on their lives.

As a renowned expert in the field of human behaviour, Arjun authored a ground-breaking book that shed light on the thrilling adventures and eye-opening discoveries of his quest. His story inspired countless individuals to question their own relationships with lies, to embrace authenticity, and to strive for a world where truth reigns supreme.

And so, the tale of Arjun stands as a testament to the power of knowledge, resilience, and the enduring pursuit of truth in a world shrouded in deception.

Lying is a complex phenomenon that can be influenced by various psychological, social, and evolutionary factors. Understanding these reasons can provide insights into why people engage in deceptive behaviours. Let's explore each of these dimensions:

Psychological Reasons:

1. Self-Protection: People may lie to protect themselves from negative consequences, punishment, or harm. It serves as a defence mechanism to shield their self-image or preserve their well-being.

2. Impression Management: Lying can be driven by the desire to create a favourable impression or maintain social status. People may embellish their achievements, fabricate stories, or present themselves in a more positive light to gain social acceptance or admiration.

3. Fear of Rejection: Individuals may lie to avoid rejection, criticism, or disapproval from others. They may alter their behaviour or present a false image to fit societal expectations or conform to social norms.

4. Personal Gain: Lying can be motivated by personal gain or material benefits. Individuals may engage in deceitful behaviours to acquire resources, manipulate situations to their advantage, or secure desired outcomes.

Social Reasons:

1. Social Harmony: Lying can be employed to maintain social harmony and avoid conflict. White lies or polite deceptions are often used to spare others' feelings or smooth interpersonal interactions.

2. Reputation Management: People may lie to manage their reputation or protect their social standing. By concealing undesirable information or presenting themselves in a more positive light, they aim to preserve their image in the eyes of others.

3. Conformity and Group Dynamics: In group settings, individuals may lie to conform to group norms, maintain cohesion, or avoid ostracism. Lying can align with the expectations and values of a particular social group, fostering a sense of belonging.

4. Self-Presentation: Lying can be a means of self-presentation, where individuals construct narratives or present themselves in ways

that align with their desired identity. This can occur in personal relationships, professional settings, or online interactions.

Evolutionary Reasons:

1. Survival and Adaptation: Evolutionary perspectives suggest that lying may have conferred survival advantages. In certain situations, deception could have increased individuals' chances of obtaining resources, securing mates, or protecting themselves from threats.

2. Strategic Interactions: Lying can be seen as part of strategic interactions, where individuals aim to outwit others for reproductive or survival benefits. This can manifest in competition for resources, mating opportunities, or social dominance.

3. Cooperative Deception: In social species, including humans, deception can be used as a cooperative strategy. By deceiving others, individuals may gain advantages within social hierarchies, secure alliances, or protect their group's interests.

4. Mentalizing Abilities: Humans possess sophisticated mentalizing abilities, allowing them to understand and predict the thoughts, intentions, and beliefs of others. Lying can be a by-product of these abilities, as individuals manipulate others' perceptions or exploit their understanding of human cognition.

It's important to note that while these reasons shed light on the motivations behind lying, not all lies are driven by malicious intent. Context, cultural factors, individual differences, and moral considerations also shape the frequency and nature of deceptive behaviours.

Chapter 4

Arjun was no ordinary individual. With an innate curiosity and a passion for unravelling the mysteries of human behaviour, he possessed a unique talent for detecting lies. From a young age, he had an uncanny ability to read people, picking up on subtle cues that revealed the truth beneath their words.

One fateful day, Arjun received a call from an old friend, Riya. She was a renowned investigative journalist working on a high-profile case that involved uncovering a web of deceit and corruption. Riya had heard of Arjun's extraordinary lie-detection skills and sought his assistance in unravelling the truth.

Intrigued by the challenge, Arjun joined Riya in her investigation. Their journey led them through a labyrinth of conspiracies, double-crosses, and hidden agendas. As they dug deeper, they encountered a network of powerful individuals determined to protect their secrets at all costs.

Armed with his keen observation skills, Arjun paid close attention to the verbal and non-verbal cues of deception. He analysed the subtle shifts in body language, the fluctuations in voice tone, and the incongruence between words and expressions. These cues served as the breadcrumbs that would lead them closer to the truth.

One of their key suspects was a charismatic businessman named Vikram. On the surface, Vikram appeared charming and trustworthy, but Arjun sensed a hidden darkness lurking beneath his facade. During their interactions with him, Arjun noticed the subtle signs of deception—a fleeting micro expression of contempt, a slight hesitation in his responses, and a tendency to groom his meticulously groomed beard when confronted with difficult questions.

As Arjun and Riya continued their investigation, they uncovered a series of intricate financial frauds linked to Vikram. However, they knew they needed concrete evidence to expose his deception and bring him to justice.

Arjun devised a plan to put Vikram's lies to the test. He arranged a meeting with Vikram under the guise of a potential business partnership. As they engaged in a conversation about their supposed venture, Arjun skillfully probed for inconsistencies, paying attention to the subtle shifts in Vikram's behaviour.

Just as Arjun suspected, Vikram's true intentions began to surface. He became increasingly evasive, his body language betraying his discomfort. Arjun skillfully maneuvered the conversation, trapping Vikram in his own web of lies.

In a thrilling turn of events, Riya managed to obtain a crucial piece of evidence that would expose Vikram's fraudulent activities. Armed with this evidence, they confronted him with the truth, shattering his carefully crafted facade.

But the story didn't end there. As they thought they had triumphed over deception, a new twist emerged. They discovered that their investigation had unknowingly led them into a much larger conspiracy—one that involved influential figures at the highest levels of society.

Suddenly, Arjun and Riya found themselves entangled in a dangerous game of cat and mouse. Their lives were at stake as they raced against time to expose the truth and bring the perpetrators to justice.

Arjun's lie-detection skills were put to the ultimate test as he navigated through a maze of deceit and danger. With each encounter, he honed his abilities, relying on both his astute observations and his unwavering intuition.

In a heart-pounding climax, Arjun and Riya managed to unravel the complex web of deception, exposing the true culprits behind the conspiracy. The truth prevailed, and justice was served.

Arjun's extraordinary journey had not only exposed the lies that had plagued society but had also reinforced his belief in the power of truth and the resilience of the human spirit. Inspired by their triumph, Arjun and Riya continued their pursuit of truth, dedicating themselves to unmasking deception wherever it lurked.

Their story became a legend, whispered in the shadows, reminding everyone that even in a world of lies, there were individuals like Arjun who possessed the extraordinary ability to see through the veil of deceit and bring forth the light of truth.

Detecting lies can be a challenging task, as skilled liars can be adept at concealing their deception. However, there are certain verbal and non-verbal cues that can provide clues and increase the likelihood of identifying dishonesty. Let's explore these cues:

Verbal Cues:

1. Inconsistencies and Contradictions: Liars often struggle to maintain consistency in their stories. They may provide conflicting details or change their narrative when questioned further.

2. Excessive Use of Qualifiers: Liars may use words and phrases that act as qualifiers to distance themselves from their lies. Examples include "I think," "probably," or "as far as I remember."

3. Unnecessarily Detailed Responses: Liars often try to compensate for their deception by providing excessive and unnecessary details. This can be an attempt to make their story sound more convincing.

4. Delayed or Stalled Responses: When faced with unexpected questions, liars may stall for time to come up with a plausible response. They may hesitate, repeat the question, or ask for clarification.

5. Lack of Spontaneity: Truthful individuals typically provide immediate and spontaneous responses. Liars, on the other hand, may appear more calculated and rehearsed in their answers.

Non-Verbal Cues:

1. Body Language: Liars may display signs of discomfort, such as fidgeting, avoiding eye contact, or adopting defensive postures. They may also engage in self-soothing behaviours like touching their face or crossing their arms.

2. Micro expressions: These fleeting facial expressions can reveal true emotions that contradict a liar's words. Micro expressions include brief flashes of fear, surprise, or contempt, which can be difficult to conceal.

3. Incongruence between Verbal and Non-Verbal Cues: When someone's words do not align with their body language, it can indicate deception. For example, a person saying "I'm fine" with a forced smile and tense posture.

4. Changes in Voice: Liars may experience vocal changes, such as higher pitch, increased stuttering, or a sudden decrease in volume. These changes can reflect anxiety and discomfort associated with deception.

5. Grooming Behaviours: Lying can induce stress, leading to unconscious grooming behaviours like touching the face, adjusting clothing, or playing with objects. These actions can indicate heightened nervousness.

It's important to note that these cues are not fool proof indicators of deception, as individuals may exhibit some of these behaviours due to other factors like anxiety or discomfort in specific situations. Additionally, cultural and individual differences can influence the expression of these cues.

To enhance lie detection, it is beneficial to establish a baseline of an individual's normal behaviour and communication patterns. This baseline allows for better identification of deviations that may signal deception. Additionally, paying attention to clusters of cues rather than relying solely on isolated cues can provide a more accurate assessment.

It's worth mentioning that lie detection is a complex skill that requires training and expertise. Professionals such as forensic psychologists and law enforcement officers undergo specialized training to improve their ability to detect deception.

Chapter 5

Arjun, a young man with an insatiable thirst for knowledge and a keen interest in human behaviour, found himself captivated by the intricate interplay of lies and their consequences. He yearned to explore the depths of this complex phenomenon and understand how it impacted various aspects of our lives.

Arjun embarked on a journey of self-discovery, delving into the world of lies with unwavering determination. He had always been observant and perceptive, capable of discerning the subtlest cues in human behaviour. With this innate ability, he set out to unravel the profound effects of deception.

As Arjun ventured into the realm of relationships, he witnessed first-hand the destructive power of lying on trust. He encountered individuals whose lives had been shattered by betrayal, their once-solid foundations crumbling beneath the weight of deceit. The emotional turmoil he witnessed left an indelible mark on his soul, fuelling his quest for understanding.

In his quest, Arjun met Maya, a young woman whose heart had been bruised by the corrosive effects of lying. Maya had trusted blindly, only to be met with a web of lies that tore their relationship apart. Her experience echoed the stories of countless others, and Arjun was determined to bring light to their pain.

Together, Arjun and Maya embarked on a mission to delve deeper into the consequences of lying. They sought out experts in psychology, engaging in deep conversations that uncovered the intricate web of emotions tied to deception. The impact on self-esteem became apparent as they spoke with individuals who had been stripped of their confidence, haunted by the guilt and shame of their deceitful actions.

Arjun and Maya also explored the toll that lying took on mental health. They encountered individuals, whose lives were consumed by anxiety and stress, constantly living in fear of their lies being exposed. The weight of their deception burdened their minds, leading to a decline in overall happiness and well-being.

As Arjun and Maya continued their exploration, they realized the profound connection between lying and authenticity. They met individuals who had lost touch with their true selves, trapped behind masks of deception. These individuals yearned for freedom, craving the ability to live their lives authentically and reconnect with their core values.

Their journey also revealed the social repercussions of lying. Arjun and Maya encountered individuals who had become social outcasts, their reputation tarnished by their dishonesty. The erosion of trust had severed ties, leaving them isolated and alone. The profound loneliness they experienced served as a stark reminder of the importance of honesty in building and maintaining meaningful connections.

Throughout their journey, Arjun and Maya grappled with their own vulnerabilities. They discovered that even they were not immune to the temptations of lying. The allure of deceit lurked in the shadows, testing their commitment to truth. It was a constant battle, a reminder that the consequences of lying were not confined to others but could also impact their own lives.

Arjun and Maya emerged from their exploration with a newfound understanding. They realized that honesty was not just a virtue but a powerful force for personal growth and the preservation of relationships. Armed with this knowledge, they became advocates for transparency, spreading awareness of the consequences of lying and encouraging others to embrace truth as a guiding principle.

Their journey had transformed them, deepening their empathy and reinforcing their commitment to living with integrity. Arjun and Maya recognized that the path of honesty was not always easy, but it was essential for personal and collective well-being. They vowed to continue their mission, to share their experiences, and to inspire others to embrace the transformative power of truth.

As Arjun and Maya's story spread, their message resonated with people from all walks of life. The ripple effect of their exploration touched countless souls, igniting a movement toward a more honest and compassionate world.

And so, the tale of Arjun and Maya serves as a reminder that the consequences of lying are far-reaching. They impact our relationships, self-esteem, and mental health, leaving behind a trail of broken trust and shattered souls. But within the darkness, there is hope—a glimmer of light that guides us toward the path of honesty, authenticity, and ultimately, personal liberation.

Lying carries a multitude of consequences that can significantly impact various aspects of our lives, including relationships, self-esteem, and mental health. Let's delve into these effects:

1. Relationship Trust: Trust forms the foundation of any healthy relationship. When lies are introduced, trust is eroded. Lying creates a sense of betrayal and can lead to broken relationships, as the deceived individual may struggle to regain trust. It can cause emotional pain, resentment, and a breakdown in communication.

2. Emotional Distance: Lying creates barriers between people. When someone lies, it undermines the authenticity and intimacy in a relationship. The deceived person may feel emotionally distant, guarded, and reluctant to open up, fearing further deception. This can lead to a decline in emotional connection and overall relationship satisfaction.

3. Self-Esteem: Engaging in dishonesty can have detrimental effects on one's self-esteem. When we lie, we are essentially presenting an altered version of ourselves, which can lead to feelings of guilt, shame, and a sense of inadequacy. Over time, this can erode self-confidence and self-worth, affecting our overall well-being.

4. Mental Health: The psychological impact of lying can be significant. Constantly maintaining a façade and living with the fear of being discovered can lead to increased stress, anxiety, and emotional

distress. Lying can also contribute to a cycle of guilt and remorse, impacting mental health and causing a decline in overall happiness.

5. Integrity and Authenticity: Lying compromises our sense of integrity and authenticity. When we engage in deception, we deviate from our values and principles, creating internal conflicts. Living a life filled with lies can lead to a loss of self-identity and a disconnection from our true selves.

6. Social Repercussions: Lies have consequences beyond individual relationships. When lies are exposed or discovered, it can damage reputations and lead to social isolation. Others may perceive the individual as untrustworthy, affecting their personal and professional relationships.

7. Escalation of Deception: Lies often require more lies to maintain the initial deception. This can create a vicious cycle of escalating dishonesty, making it increasingly challenging to untangle the web of deceit. The more lies one tells, the deeper they become entangled in their own falsehoods, leading to further complications and potential exposure.

It is important to note that the consequences of lying can vary depending on the severity and frequency of deception, as well as the individuals involved. Some lies may have minor repercussions, while others can cause irreparable damage.

To foster healthier relationships and promote well-being, it is crucial to cultivate a culture of honesty, openness, and vulnerability. Building trust through transparent communication and embracing authenticity can help create stronger connections and preserve mental and emotional well-being.

Remember, choosing honesty not only benefits our relationships but also contributes to our own self-growth, fostering a sense of integrity and a healthier state of mind.

Chapter 6

Raj, his eight-year-old son, was the object of his adoring care. Arjun was a strong believer in the value of honesty and wished to impart it in his young kid. He set out on a mission to impart this significant virtue since he was aware that teaching honesty was essential for Raj's moral and social growth.

Arjun understood that leading by example was the most effective way to teach honesty. He made a conscious effort to be truthful in his words and actions. Even when faced with challenging situations, he never compromised his integrity. He admitted his own mistakes and shortcomings, showing Raj that everyone can make errors, but honesty is essential for growth and trust.

Creating a safe and non-judgmental environment was another strategy Arjun employed. He encouraged open communication and assured Raj that honesty was valued more than avoiding consequences. Arjun wanted his son to feel comfortable expressing himself honestly, knowing that his thoughts and feelings would be respected.

Whenever Raj displayed honesty, Arjun made sure to reinforce his positive behaviour. He praised and appreciated Raj for his truthfulness, emphasizing how it built trust and strengthened their relationship. Through his encouragement, Arjun hoped to foster a sense of pride and satisfaction in Raj for choosing honesty.

Understanding the consequences of lying was crucial for Raj's development. Arjun took the time to explain to his son how lies could hurt others and damage relationships. They discussed the importance of trust and how lies could erode that trust, impacting both the liar and the person deceived. Arjun wanted Raj to comprehend the significance of honesty and the integrity it brought to one's character.

To cultivate empathy, Arjun guided Raj to consider how lying could hurt others. They engaged in discussions about empathy, encouraging Raj to imagine how he would feel if someone lied to him. Arjun wanted his son to develop a deep understanding of the emotional impact lies could have on people's lives, reinforcing the importance of honesty in building strong and caring relationships.

Arjun established clear expectations about honesty, explaining why it was important in their family. They discussed the values and principles that guided their actions, highlighting how honesty aligned with their beliefs. Arjun wanted Raj to understand that honesty was not just a personal choice but a reflection of their shared values.

In teaching problem-solving and conflict resolution, Arjun provided Raj with alternative strategies to handle difficult situations. He taught Raj the importance of effective communication, active listening, and negotiation skills. Arjun wanted his son to understand that there were better ways to resolve conflicts than resorting to lies, emphasizing the power of honest dialogue.

When Raj made a mistake and lied, Arjun created space for reflection and discussion. Instead of immediately punishing him, Arjun calmly addressed the behaviour. He asked Raj to think about the reasons behind his dishonesty and helped him understand the impact it had on trust and their relationship. Arjun guided Raj to reflect on how he could have handled the situation differently with honesty and integrity.

Arjun reinforced trust-building behaviours by teaching Raj the significance of keeping promises, being reliable, and demonstrating honesty in their daily interactions. He encouraged Raj to understand that trust was built through consistent honest actions, establishing a solid foundation for meaningful relationships.

If Raj was caught in a lie, Arjun corrected and redirected his behaviour. Instead of labelling him as a "liar," Arjun focused on the behaviour itself. He explained the importance of telling the truth and engaged Raj in discussions about alternative ways he could have handled the situation with honesty and openness.

Teaching problem-solving and responsibility was also vital in Arjun's approach. He encouraged Raj to take responsibility for his actions and find constructive solutions to rectify any harm caused by his lies. Arjun encouraged Raj to apologize and make amends when appropriate, helping him understand the importance of repairing relationships damaged by dishonesty.

Throughout their journey, Arjun maintained open communication with Raj. He created an environment where Raj felt safe to approach him with his mistakes, fears, and uncertainties. Arjun actively listened to Raj's thoughts and concerns, providing guidance and support without judgment. He wanted Raj to know that honesty was not only expected but also celebrated in their home.

As the years went by, Arjun witnessed the growth of his son. Raj embraced honesty as a core value, understanding its importance in building relationships, preserving self-integrity, and navigating life's challenges. Arjun's efforts had paid off, and he was proud to see Raj embody the virtue of honesty in all aspects of his life.

Arjun and Raj's story serves as a reminder that teaching honesty is an on-going journey. It requires patience, consistency, and understanding. Each child is unique, and their understanding of honesty will develop over time. By employing these strategies and nurturing a supportive environment, parents can guide their children toward a path of integrity, trust, and personal growth.

Teaching honesty to children is an essential part of their moral and social development. By instilling a strong foundation of truthfulness, we equip children with the tools to navigate relationships and make ethical choices. Here are some strategies to promote honesty and address lying behaviour:

1. Lead by Example: Children learn by observing their parents and caregivers. Model honesty in your own words and actions, as children are more likely to emulate behaviours they see. Be truthful, even when it's difficult, and admit your own mistakes or shortcomings.

2. Create a Safe and Non-Judgmental Environment: Foster an environment where children feel comfortable expressing themselves honestly without fear of harsh punishment or judgment. Encourage open communication and assure them that you value honesty over avoiding consequences.

3. Reinforce Positive Behaviour: Praise and reinforce honesty whenever you observe it. Acknowledge and appreciate their truthfulness, emphasizing the importance of telling the truth and the trust it builds in relationships.

4. Teach the Consequences of Lying: Help children understand the negative consequences of lying, both for themselves and others. Discuss the potential harm it can cause to relationships, loss of trust, and the impact on their own integrity and self-esteem.

5. Encourage Empathy: Foster empathy by helping children understands how lying can hurt others. Encourage them to consider how they would feel if someone lied to them and how honesty can strengthen relationships.

6. Establish Clear Expectations: Set clear expectations about honesty and explain why it is important. Discuss the values and principles that guide your family and how honesty aligns with those values.

7. Problem-Solving and Conflict Resolution: Teach children alternative strategies to handle difficult situations or conflicts that may tempt them to lie. Help them develop problem-solving skills, effective communication, and negotiation techniques to resolve conflicts honestly and constructively.

8. Provide Space for Reflection: When a child lies, provide an opportunity for reflection and discussion rather than immediately resorting to punishment. Encourage them to think about the reasons behind their dishonesty and help them understand the impact it has on trust and relationships.

9. Reinforce Trust-Building Behaviours: Teach children how to build trust through actions such as keeping promises, being reliable, and demonstrating honesty in small everyday situations.

10. Correct and Redirect: If a child is caught in a lie, address the behaviour calmly and assertively. Avoid labelling the child as a "liar" but instead focus on the behavior itself. Help them understand the importance of telling the truth and discuss alternative ways they could have handled the situation.

11. Encourage Problem-Solving and Responsibility: Teach children to take responsibility for their actions and find constructive solutions to rectify any harm caused by their lies. Encourage them to apologize and make amends when appropriate.

12. Maintain Open Communication: Foster an environment where children feel comfortable coming to you with their mistakes, fears, and uncertainties. Encourage open dialogue and active listening, allowing them to express their thoughts and concerns without fear of harsh judgment.

Remember, teaching honesty is an on-going process that requires patience, consistency, and understanding. Each child is unique, and their understanding of honesty will develop over time. By employing these strategies and nurturing a supportive environment, you can help children embrace honesty as a core value and guide them toward a path of integrity and trust.

Chapter 7

Arjun was well known for his unwavering truthfulness and his ability to detect fraud in a number of situations. He had a remarkable talent for finding lies in the complicated worlds of politics, journalism, business, and religion.

Arjun's keen sense of discernment had developed over the years, honed through personal experiences and a commitment to truth. He believed that honesty was the bedrock of a just society and was determined to combat falsehoods in every context.

In the realm of politics, Arjun observed the manipulative tactics used by politicians to sway public opinion. He delved deep into the world of information, seeking diverse and reliable sources to gather a comprehensive understanding of political issues. Arjun encouraged civil discourse, organizing community forums where citizens could engage in respectful discussions and challenge deceptive narratives. Through his efforts, he empowered people to question inconsistencies and hold elected officials accountable for their words and actions.

Arjun's media literacy skills were unparalleled. He had a knack for discerning between reliable and biased sources of information. He taught others to evaluate the credibility, objectivity, and accuracy of news articles, videos, and social media posts. Arjun tirelessly fact-checked information, using independent research and fact-checking websites to verify the claims made by media outlets. He urged people to diversify their media consumption, breaking free from echo chambers that reinforced pre-existing beliefs. Through his guidance, the community became more adept at recognizing sensationalized claims and separating truth from fiction.

As an entrepreneur, Arjun emphasized the importance of due diligence in business. He conducted thorough research before engaging in any transaction, verifying claims made by companies and individuals. Arjun meticulously read contracts and agreements, ensuring transparency and protecting his interests. He encouraged others to do the same, reminding them that reporting unethical behaviour and fraud was vital for maintaining integrity in the business world. His commitment to honesty and ethical practices inspired others to follow suit, leading to a more trustworthy and reputable business community.

Religion, with its complex beliefs and interpretations, was not exempt from Arjun's scrutiny. He approached religious teachings with a critical and open mind, questioning aspects that seemed questionable or contradictory. Arjun embarked on a personal exploration of different religious beliefs and traditions, seeking a broader perspective. Engaging in discussions with individuals of varying religious backgrounds, he fostered understanding and respect. Arjun emphasized the core values of compassion, empathy, and ethical behaviour that were present in most religious teachings. By focusing on these principles, he helped people navigate religious contexts with integrity and authenticity.

Arjun's unwavering commitment to truth and his ability to cope with lies in various contexts earned him respect and admiration. People sought his guidance, and his influence spread throughout Veridium. His efforts transformed the city, fostering a culture of critical thinking, responsibility, and respectful discourse.

Over time, Arjun's legacy extended beyond Veridium. His principles and strategies for dealing with lies became a guiding light for societies far and wide. People recognized the importance of personal responsibility, media literacy, and open dialogue in combating deception. Arjun's story inspired individuals across the globe to embrace honesty, seek reliable information, and engage in respectful conversations.

Arjun's journey was a testament to the power of integrity and the impact one person can have on a community. His unwavering commitment to truth not only transformed his own life but also shaped the lives of countless others. The city of Veridium, once plagued by deceit, emerged as a beacon of transparency and accountability.

And so, the tale of Arjun, the guardian of truth, became a legend whispered through the ages—a reminder that honesty and a relentless pursuit of truth can illuminate even the darkest corners of society.

Coping with lies in different contexts, such as politics, media, business, and religion, can be challenging. Here are some strategies for dealing with lies in these specific domains:

1. Politics:

- Seek diverse and reliable sources of information: Engage in critical thinking and gather information from multiple sources to gain a more comprehensive understanding of political issues. Look for reputable news outlets and fact-checking organizations.

- Hold politicians accountable: Stay informed about the actions and statements of politicians. Be an active participant in the democratic process by questioning inconsistencies and holding elected officials accountable for their words and actions.

- Engage in civil discourse: Foster open and respectful discussions about political topics. Encourage constructive dialogue and challenge misinformation or deceptive tactics while promoting understanding and empathy.

2. Media:

- Media literacy: Develop media literacy skills to discern between reliable and biased sources of information. Learn to evaluate the credibility, objectivity, and accuracy of news articles, videos, and social media posts.

- Fact-checking: Verify the information presented in media outlets by using fact-checking websites and independent research. Be cautious of sensationalized or exaggerated claims.

- Diversify your media consumption: Consume news from a variety of sources with different perspectives to gain a more balanced understanding of events. Avoid echo chambers that reinforce pre-existing beliefs.

3. Business:

- Due diligence: Conduct thorough research before engaging in business transactions. Verify claims made by companies and individuals, especially regarding products, services, and financial matters.

- Read contracts and agreements carefully: Take the time to read and understand the terms and conditions of contracts. Seek legal advice if necessary to ensure transparency and protect your interests.

- Report unethical behaviour: If you encounter dishonest practices or fraud in business, consider reporting the misconduct to relevant authorities or regulatory bodies.

4. Religion:

- Critical thinking: Approach religious teachings with a critical and open mind. Question and seek clarification on aspects that seem questionable or contradictory.

- Personal exploration: Explore different religious beliefs and traditions to gain a broader perspective. Engage in discussions with individuals of varying religious backgrounds to foster understanding and respect.

- Focus on core values: Emphasize the fundamental values of compassion, empathy, and ethical behaviour that are present in most religious teachings. Use these principles as a guide to navigate religious contexts.

In all contexts, it is essential to foster a sense of personal responsibility and critical thinking. Cultivate a habit of seeking reliable information, questioning assumptions, and engaging in respectful dialogue. By becoming informed and active participants in these domains, we can contribute to a more transparent and accountable society.

Chapter 8

Arjun was known for his wisdom and discretion. His reputation as a trustworthy and reliable confidant made him the go-to person for many villagers seeking advice or needing to share their secrets.

Arjun's ability to handle secrets with utmost care and discretion stemmed from his strong belief in the importance of trust and confidentiality. He understood that keeping secrets was not merely about respecting others' wishes but also about upholding the bonds of trust that held relationships together.

One sunny morning, as Arjun walked through the bustling village square, he noticed a commotion near the marketplace. Curiosity piqued, he hurried toward the crowd to discover what had caused the uproar. In the midst of the chaos, he spotted his childhood friend, Ravi, looking distressed.

Arjun approached Ravi and asked, "What's the matter, my friend? Why is everyone so agitated?"

Ravi sighed heavily and confided in Arjun, "I have stumbled upon a secret that could disrupt the harmony of our village. It involves the village head, Gopal. He has been involved in corrupt practices, misusing his power for personal gain."

Arjun listened attentively, his mind racing with thoughts on how to handle this delicate situation. He knew that the revelation of such a secret could have far-reaching consequences for the village and its inhabitants.

Remembering the considerations for handling secrets, Arjun carefully weighed the factors at play. Safety and well-being were paramount, and if Gopal's actions posed a threat to the villagers, it was crucial to prioritize their welfare. Additionally, the ethical considerations demanded that he take a stand against corruption and uphold the values of honesty and justice.

Arjun approached Ravi and said, "My friend, the secret you shared with me carries great significance. It involves the safety and well-being of our fellow villagers. We cannot ignore this, but we must handle it with utmost care."

Together, Arjun and Ravi devised a plan to gather evidence and document Gopal's corrupt practices discreetly. They knew that revealing the truth without substantial proof would only lead to distrust and accusations.

Days turned into weeks as Arjun and Ravi worked tirelessly, collecting evidence, speaking to witnesses, and documenting every detail meticulously. Their dedication and determination earned them the support of other villagers who had long suspected Gopal's dishonesty.

Finally, armed with undeniable proof, Arjun and Ravi decided to approach the village council. They presented their findings, allowing the truth to unfold before the eyes of the villagers and the council members.

The revelation of Gopal's deceit sent shockwaves through the village. The council, recognizing the gravity of the situation, took swift action, removing Gopal from his position and initiating an investigation into his actions.

In the aftermath of this revelation, the village went through a period of introspection and healing. The trust that had been eroded by Gopal's corruption slowly began to rebuild. Arjun's role in this transformation was acknowledged by the villagers, who praised his wisdom and integrity.

Arjun, however, remained humble, understanding that his actions were guided by the considerations of handling secrets responsibly. He had upheld trust, prioritized safety and well-being, and ensured that the impact on others was carefully considered.

In the years that followed, Arjun's reputation as a trusted confidant grew even stronger. Villagers sought his guidance, not only to share their secrets but also to seek advice on how to navigate the complexities of life with honesty and integrity.

Arjun's story became a reminder to all that handling secrets required a delicate balance of trust, safety, ethics, impact, intentions, consent, and cultural norms. It taught the villagers the importance of upholding these in their everyday lives, fostering a community built on transparency, compassion, and trust.

And so, the village of Amrita Nagar continued to thrive, guided by the wisdom of Arjun and the understanding that handling secrets with care was an integral part of building a harmonious and honest society.

Handling secrets and deciding when to keep or reveal information can be a delicate balancing act. Here are some considerations to guide us in navigating this complex terrain:

1. Trust and Confidentiality: Respecting the trust placed in us is paramount. If someone confides in us and explicitly asks us to keep a secret, it is important to honour their trust unless there are compelling reasons to do otherwise. Breaking confidentiality can damage relationships and erode trust.

2. Safety and Well-being: When information involves the safety or well-being of someone, it may be necessary to disclose it. If someone's physical, emotional, or mental health is at risk, it is crucial to prioritize their welfare over keeping a secret. Safety should always take precedence.

3. Legal and Ethical Considerations: If keeping a secret would involve engaging in illegal or unethical activities, it is essential to reassess the situation. Upholding the law and adhering to ethical principles should guide our decision-making process.

4. Context and Impact: Consider the potential consequences of keeping or revealing information. Reflect on the impact it may have on individuals involved, relationships, and the broader community. Weigh the potential benefits and drawbacks before making a decision.

5. Intentions and Motivations: Examine your intentions for wanting to reveal or keep information. If the motivation is rooted in personal gain, revenge, or malice, it may be necessary to revaluate the situation. Transparency and honesty should be guided by genuine concern, empathy, and a desire for the greater good.

6. Consent and Ownership: Respect individuals' autonomy and their right to control the information they share. Seek permission before revealing personal or sensitive details, ensuring that the individuals involved are comfortable with the disclosure.

7. Impact on Others: Consider how the revelation of information may impact others who are not directly involved. Will it cause unnecessary harm or disrupt relationships? Strive to strike a balance between truth and the potential consequences on others.

8. Cultural and Social Norms: Be mindful of cultural and social norms that may influence the handling of secrets. Different cultures and communities may have varying expectations regarding secrecy and disclosure. Understanding and respecting these norms can guide our decision-making process.

Ultimately, each situation is unique, and there is no one-size-fits-all approach. It requires careful thought, empathy, and a consideration of the values and principles that guide our lives. Strive to find a balance that respects confidentiality, prioritizes safety and well-being, upholds legal and ethical standards, and fosters open and honest communication.

Chapter 9

Arjun and Kavya was a young couple deeply in love. They had been together for several years and shared a strong bond built on trust and honesty. However, as their relationship progressed, Arjun started noticing a pattern in Kavya's behaviour. She would often tell little white lies about insignificant things, and it seemed to be happening more frequently.

At first, Arjun dismissed it as harmless fibbing. But as time went on, he realized that Kavya's lies were becoming more frequent and more elaborate. It was as if she couldn't resist the urge to make up stories, even when there was no apparent reason to do so.

Concerned for Kavya's well-being, Arjun decided to research her behaviour. He came across information about pathological and compulsive lying disorders. The signs he read about matched Kavya's behaviour perfectly - the consistent pattern of lying, the difficulty distinguishing truth from fiction, and the impulsivity behind her lies.

Determined to help Kavya, Arjun approached the situation with care and empathy. He knew that accusing her or judging her would only push her away. Instead, he created a safe space for open and honest communication, encouraging Kavya to reflect on her lying behaviour without fear of judgment.

One evening, as they sat together on their favourite park bench, Arjun broached the subject gently. "Kavya, I've noticed that you've been telling lies lately, even about the smallest things. I want you to know that I'm here to support you, and I want to understand what's going on. Can we talk about it?"

Kavya initially seemed defensive, but she could sense the sincerity and love in Arjun's words. She took a deep breath and admitted that she had been struggling with her lying behaviour. She explained how she felt an overwhelming compulsion to lie, even when she knew it was unnecessary or harmful. She shared her fears and insecurities, revealing that lying had become a way for her to protect herself and enhance her self-image.

Arjun listened attentively, validating Kavya's feelings and assuring her that he was there to support her unconditionally. He gently suggested that seeking professional help might provide a way forward.

Together, they researched therapists who specialized in cognitive-behavioural therapy (CBT), known to be effective in treating pathological and compulsive lying disorders.

With Arjun's support, Kavya found the courage to schedule an appointment with a qualified therapist. In therapy, she delved into the underlying causes of her lying behaviour and learned strategies to challenge her distorted thought patterns. Through CBT, she developed healthier coping mechanisms and gained a better understanding of the impact her lies had on her life and relationships.

Alongside therapy, Kavya also attended support group meetings where she connected with others who were going through similar struggles. The support group provided her with a sense of community and understanding, offering valuable guidance and encouragement throughout her recovery journey.

Arjun stood by Kavya's side every step of the way, celebrating her progress and offering unwavering support. He understood that overcoming a pathological or compulsive lying disorder would take time and patience. There were setbacks along the way, but together they learned to navigate through them with resilience and compassion.

Over time, Kavya's lying diminished as she gained control over her compulsions. The trust between Arjun and Kavya grew stronger than ever before, founded on their shared commitment to honesty and understanding. They became advocates for mental health, spreading awareness about pathological and compulsive lying disorders and helping others find the support they needed.

Arjun and Kavya's journey was a testament to the power of love, empathy, and professional help in overcoming the challenges associated with pathological and compulsive lying disorders.

Through their shared experience, they not only strengthened their relationship but also inspired hope and healing in others facing similar struggles.

Lies can sometimes be a symptom of underlying problems or psychological disorders. It is important to recognize and provide support to individuals who may be struggling with pathological or compulsive lying disorders. Here are some signs to look out for and steps to help them:

1. Consistent Pattern of Lying: Pathological or compulsive liars tend to engage in a persistent and habitual pattern of lying. They may lie about both significant and trivial matters, often without any apparent reason or benefit.

2. Difficulty Distinguishing Truth from Fiction: Individuals with lying disorders may have difficulty distinguishing between reality and their own fabrications. They may genuinely believe their lies and struggle to recognize the truth.

3. Impulsivity and Compulsivity: Pathological liars often feel an intense urge to lie, even when it is unnecessary or may cause harm. They may lie impulsively, without considering the consequences or impact on others.

4. Emotional Distress and Low Self-Esteem: Some individuals who engage in compulsive lying may experience emotional distress and low self-esteem. They may use lying as a coping mechanism to protect them or enhance their self-image.

5. Seek Professional Help: If you suspect someone may have a pathological or compulsive lying disorder, encourage them to seek professional help from a qualified mental health professional. A therapist or counsellor can provide an accurate diagnosis and develop an appropriate treatment plan.

6. Be Supportive and Non-Judgmental: It is crucial to approach the person with compassion, empathy, and understanding. Avoid criticizing or accusing them of lying, as this may further exacerbate their distress. Instead, create a safe and non-judgmental space where they feel comfortable opening up about their struggles.

7. Encourage Self-Reflection and Awareness: Help the person develop self-awareness by encouraging them to reflect on their lying behaviour and its impact on their life and relationships. This can help them gain insight into the underlying issues driving their compulsion to lie.

8. Cognitive-Behavioural Therapy (CBT): CBT is a commonly used therapeutic approach for treating pathological and compulsive lying disorders. It focuses on identifying and challenging distorted thought patterns and developing healthier coping mechanisms. Encourage the individual to consider this type of therapy as an effective treatment option.

9. Support Groups: Support groups, such as those specifically designed for individuals with compulsive lying disorders, can provide a sense of community and understanding. Encourage the person to explore these resources as they can offer valuable support and guidance.

10. Patience and Understanding: Overcoming a pathological or compulsive lying disorder is a journey that requires time, patience, and commitment. Be supportive throughout their recovery process and understand that setbacks may occur. Celebrate their progress and offer encouragement along the way.

It is important to note that diagnosing and treating pathological or compulsive lying disorders should be done by qualified professionals. While you can provide support, it is ultimately up to the individual to seek professional help and actively engage in their own recovery.

Chapter 10

One sunny morning, as Arjun made his way through the bustling streets, he noticed a commotion near the marketplace. Curiosity piqued, he approached the gathering to find a distraught woman named Kavitha at the centre of the crowd. Tearfully, Kavitha revealed that her trusted friend and business partner had deceived her, resulting in significant financial losses for both of them.

Arjun's compassionate heart compelled him to help Kavitha in her time of need. He approached her and offered his support, lending an empathetic ear to her story. As Kavitha poured her heart out, Arjun listened attentively, acknowledging and validating her feelings of hurt and betrayal.

Recognizing the importance of open communication, Arjun encouraged Kavitha to confront her friend directly and express her emotions honestly. Together, they crafted a plan to engage in a calm and respectful dialogue, allowing both parties to be heard and understood.

Armed with courage and determination, Kavitha confronted her friend, who expressed remorse for the lies and deception. It became clear that fear and insecurity had driven the friend's actions, clouding their judgment. Arjun, ever the advocate of seeking understanding, urged Kavitha to empathize with her friend's struggles, recognizing that the lies were symptoms of deeper pain.

With a sincere desire to rebuild trust, Kavitha 's friend took responsibility for their actions, acknowledging the hurt they had caused. Arjun emphasized the importance of rebuilding honesty, stressing the need for transparency and accountability moving forward. Together, they established clear boundaries to protect Kavitha 's interests and gradually rebuild the trust that had been shattered.

Patience became their guiding light as forgiveness and healing unfolded. Arjun advised Kavitha to engage in self-reflection, encouraging her to focus on personal growth and self-care. He reminded her that forgiveness was a personal journey and that time was an essential ingredient in rebuilding trust.

Recognizing the significance of support, Arjun introduced Kavitha to a trusted counsellor who specialized in guiding individuals through the process of forgiveness and rebuilding relationships. The counsellor provided Kavitha with guidance, perspective, and a safe space to process her emotions.

As months passed, Kavitha embarked on a transformative journey. Through the support of Arjun, the counsellor, and her own resilience, she learned to navigate the complexities of forgiveness. She embraced the opportunity for personal growth, recognizing her own vulnerabilities and areas for improvement.

Kavitha's friend, too, demonstrated genuine remorse and a commitment to change. They consistently upheld their newfound honesty, working together to rectify the financial losses and rebuild trust in their partnership.

In time, the wounds began to heal, and the bond between Kavitha and her friend grew stronger than ever before. Their story became a testament to the power of forgiveness, resilience, and the capacity for growth in the face of deception.

Arjun, the hero of this tale, stood as a beacon of hope and compassion, guiding Kavitha and her friend toward forgiveness and the restoration of their once-precious relationship. His unwavering belief in the process of healing and the power of forgiveness had truly made a difference in their lives.

And so, the city witnessed the remarkable journey of forgiveness, a testament to the strength of the human spirit and the transformative power of second chances. It was a reminder that forgiveness and rebuilding trust were not mere ideals but tangible pathways to healing and growth.

Forgiving lies and rebuilding trust can be a challenging and complex process, but it is possible with time, patience, and open communication. Here are some steps to help in forgiving lies and rebuilding trust:

1. Acknowledge and Validate Your Feelings: Recognize and acknowledge the emotions you are experiencing, such as hurt, anger, or betrayal. Allow yourself to feel these emotions and validate them without judgment.

2. Communicate Openly: Engage in open and honest communication with the person who lied to you or whom you lied to. Express your feelings and concerns, and encourage them to do the same. Create a safe space for dialogue where both parties can be heard and understood.

3. Seek Understanding: Try to understand the reasons behind the lie. Was it a mistake? Was it out of fear or insecurity? Understanding the underlying motivations can help provide context and foster empathy.

4. Take Responsibility: If you were the one who lied, take responsibility for your actions. Acknowledge the hurt you caused and express genuine remorse. Take steps to rectify the situation and demonstrate your commitment to change.

5. Rebuild Honesty: Rebuilding trust requires a commitment to honesty moving forward. Be transparent in your words and actions, and strive to consistently tell the truth. This includes being accountable for your mistakes and addressing any issues that arise promptly and honestly.

6. Set Boundaries: Establish clear boundaries to protect yourself and rebuild trust gradually. These boundaries may include increased transparency, open access to communication devices, or additional checks and balances to ensure accountability.

7. Patience and Time: Forgiving lies and rebuilding trust takes time. Healing is a process that cannot be rushed. Be patient with yourself and the other person, allowing the necessary time for trust to be rebuilt organically.

8. Seek Support: If the impact of the lie is significant or if you're finding it challenging to move forward, consider seeking support from

a trusted friend, family member, or therapist. They can provide guidance, perspective, and a safe space to process your emotions.

9. Focus on Personal Growth: Use the experience as an opportunity for personal growth and self-reflection. Reflect on your own vulnerabilities and areas for improvement. Engage in self-care activities that promote healing and emotional well-being.

10. Give Second Chances: Forgiveness does not mean forgetting, but it involves giving the person another chance to earn your trust. Be open to the possibility of rebuilding the relationship if the other person demonstrates genuine remorse, takes responsibility, and shows consistent change over time.

Remember that forgiveness is a personal choice, and the timeline for healing varies for each individual and situation. It may not always be possible or advisable to rebuild trust in certain circumstances. Trust should be earned through consistent actions over time, and it's important to prioritize your emotional well-being throughout the process.

Part 2

In the captivating journey that lies ahead, we have embarked on a profound exploration of the impact and significance of lies in human life. Part I of our voyage, encompassing ten enthralling chapters, immersed us in the intricate web of lies through compelling stories and powerful takeaways. Now, as we transition into Part II, we delve even deeper into the realm of deception, traversing the vast landscapes of research and real-world analysis.

With each turn of the page, we leave behind the anecdotal and venture into the realm of scientific inquiry. Part II invites us to navigate the labyrinth of research, drawing upon the wealth of knowledge and insights amassed by experts in psychology, neuroscience, sociology, and biology. Together, we will unravel the layers of deception that shape our world, shedding light on the intricate mechanisms that underlie our human behaviour.

Within the vast expanse of this section, we encounter studies that dissect the cognitive processes and neural pathways engaged in the act of lying. We explore ground-breaking experiments that reveal the subtle intricacies of deception, exposing the hidden truths that lie beneath our outward facades. As we immerse ourselves in the world of research, we gain a deeper understanding of the motivations, strategies, and consequences that accompany the intricate dance of deception.

But our journey does not end with sterile laboratory findings. We traverse beyond the confines of controlled experiments, venturing into the realm of real-world contexts. Part II paints a vivid tapestry of societal dynamics, uncovering how lies permeate our political systems, economic structures, and interpersonal relationships. We dissect the webs of deception spun by those in positions of power, examining the impact of falsehoods on the fabric of our society.

As we navigate this realm of analysis, we encounter tales of whistle-blowers who defy the status quo, individuals who dare to challenge the narratives of deception woven by the powerful. We delve into historical events that have shaped the course of nations, unravelling the threads of deceit that have altered the trajectory of human history. Through these captivating narratives and in-depth analyses, we gain a panoramic view of the profound impact lies have on the world around us.

But amidst the darkness, we also uncover glimmers of hope. Part II unveils the remarkable stories of truth-seekers and truth-tellers who strive to unravel the complexities of deception. We encounter researchers who dedicate their lives to unearthing the truth, advocates who fight for transparency and justice, and individuals who dare to live authentically, breaking free from the chains of self-deception.

Through this journey of research and analysis, we are invited to challenge our preconceptions and question the narratives that shape our understanding of reality. We are encouraged to view deception through a critical lens, to discern the subtle nuances and hidden agendas that underlie the stories we are told. Armed with knowledge and insight, we can navigate the complex landscapes of truth and lies with wisdom and discernment.

So, dear reader, as we venture forth into the realms of research and real-world analysis, prepares to be captivated by the depth and breadth of knowledge that awaits you. Through the fusion of scientific inquiry, compelling narratives, and profound insights, we will navigate the labyrinth of deception and emerge with a heightened awareness of the complexities of human behaviour.

Let us embark on this transformative journey together, as we unravel the truths that lie beneath the surface of our existence. With each chapter, we inch closer to a deeper understanding of ourselves, our interactions with others, and the intricate dance between truth and deception that shapes the very essence of our being. Embrace the adventure that awaits in Part II, and let the pursuit of truth guide us to new horizons of self-discovery and enlightenment.

Chapter 11

Deception, a captivating and mysterious phenomenon, intricately entangles itself within the intricate webs of human communication, creating a complex tapestry that obscures truth and blurs the lines between what is real and what is fictional. This essay aims to delve deep into the multifaceted nature of deception, peeling back its layers to uncover its true essence. By placing our attention on the intentions behind deception, the content that comprises it, and the context in which it occurs, we embark on a journey to explore the captivating world of deception and the profound effects it has on both individuals and societies as a whole.

Deception, like a skilled weaver, intricately intertwines itself within the very fabric of human communication. It plays with our perceptions and understanding of reality, making it difficult to discern what is true and what is false. By shining a light on its many dimensions, we aim to unravel its intricate nature and shed light on its profound implications.

By examining the intentions that drive deception, we gain insight into the motivations behind the act of deceiving others. Whether it is driven by benevolence, aiming to protect the emotions and well-being of others through well-intentioned lies, or by selfish desires, manipulating and exploiting others for personal gain, understanding these intentions allows us to comprehend the complexity of deception and its diverse manifestations.

The content of deception is equally intriguing, as lies are meticulously crafted with a blend of truth and fiction. They can take various forms, ranging from elaborate fabrications to partial truths carefully constructed to serve the deceiver's purpose. Additionally, the art of omission, deliberately leaving out certain information, adds another layer of manipulation to the content of deception. Exploring the captivating content of deception allows us to grasp the delicate balance between what is revealed and what remains concealed, highlighting the intricate nature of this deceptive art.

Context plays a crucial role in understanding the dynamics of deception. Deception can infiltrate personal relationships, social interactions, and even the corridors of power. It has the potential to fracture intimate connections, challenge authenticity in social dynamics, and serve as a potent weapon in politics and business. By examining the contextual dimensions of deception, we gain a deeper understanding of how it operates within different spheres, shedding light on its intricacies and the far-reaching consequences it can have.

The aftermath of deception is profound, as it ripples through trust, tarnishes reputations, and fractures relationships. Both the deceiver and the deceived are left grappling with the repercussions of deception, which can leave lasting doubts and suspicions. Understanding the profound consequences of deception on individuals and societies allows us to comprehend its impact on our collective well-being and the fragility of the connections that hold us together.

Ultimately, deception reflects the intricate tapestry of human existence, encompassing our desires, fears, and vulnerabilities. It challenges our morality and integrity, inviting us to question, reflect upon, and gain a deeper understanding of ourselves and those around us. By unravelling the complexities of deception, we embark on a journey of self-discovery and introspection, seeking to navigate the blurred boundaries between truth and falsehood, and fostering a society built on trust, transparency, and genuine connections.

The essence of deception is woven by a multitude of intentions that shape its intricate tapestry. Within this web of lies, we find a range of motivations that drive individuals to deceive others. Some lies are born out of a genuine desire to protect the well-being and emotions of others, giving rise to what is often referred to as "white lies." These carefully crafted falsehoods act as delicate shields, preserving harmony and safeguarding relationships. The intention behind these lies stems from a place of benevolence, where the deceiver aims to spare others from potential harm or distress.

In contrast, there exist lies fuelled by selfish desires that serve the deceiver's personal agenda. These deceptive acts manipulate and exploit others, undermining trust and compromising the authenticity of relationships. The motivations behind such lies are driven by self-interest, often seeking personal gain, power, or control. Unlike the protective nature of white lies, these self-serving deceptions disregard the well-being of others and prioritize the deceiver's own needs.

By exploring the diverse intentions that underlie deception, we gain valuable insights into the complex motivations that give birth to deceit. Understanding the intentions behind lies allows us to comprehend the underlying dynamics of human behaviour and the complexities of interpersonal relationships. It also provides a window into the moral implications associated with deception, as the intentions behind lies can shape the ethical boundaries within which they are perceived.

Deception encompasses a wide range of actions, whether they are small or significant, cruel or kind, all aimed at persuading others to believe false information. Lying is a familiar form of deception where someone deliberately states something they know to be untrue with the intention of deceiving others. For example, imagine a situation where a friend invites you to their dinner party and asks for your opinion on their casserole dish. Even though you found it repulsive, you respond with a clever dodge, saying, "Wow! I've never tasted anything like that before," cunningly implying that you enjoyed the meal without actually uttering any false statements.

Now, let's delve into four types of liars:

1. Deceitful: These individuals engage in deceitful behaviour, intentionally misleading others through lies and falsehoods.

2. Duplicitous: Duplicitous people are characterized by their tendency to present two-faced or contradictory information, often for personal gain or to manipulate others.

3. Delusional: Delusional liars genuinely believe in the false information they convey, even though it may be completely detached from reality.

4. Demoralized: These liars resort to deceit as a result of feeling disheartened or demotivated, possibly due to personal circumstances or negative experiences.

There are various categories of lies that people employ:

1. Lies of Denial: This type of lie involves an individual, whether truthful or untruthful, simply stating that they were not involved in a particular situation.

2. Lies of Omission: These lies occur when someone intentionally withholds certain information without explicitly stating anything false.

3. Lies of Fabrication: These lies involve inventing completely false information and presenting it as if it were true.

4. Lies of Minimization: In this case, the liar downplays or diminishes the significance or impact of certain facts or events.

5. Lies of Exaggeration: Here, the liar embellishes or amplifies certain details or aspects of a situation beyond their actual extent.

Lying is considered morally wrong for two primary reasons. Firstly, it corrupts an essential aspect of our humanity, namely our ability to freely and rationally make choices. Each lie we tell contradicts the part of us that possesses moral worth. Secondly, lies infringe upon the freedom of others to make rational decisions, as they are deceived by false information.

To qualify as lying, two conditions must be met: the intention to deceive and the addressee's belief in the untruthful statement. Lying requires a person to knowingly make a false statement to another individual with the intention of leading that person to believe the falsehood as true.

There are two primary methods of lying: concealment and falsification. In concealment, the liar withholds certain information without explicitly stating anything false. In falsification, the liar goes a step further by not only withholding true information but also presenting false information as if it were true.

However, one of the most common motivations for telling lies is to avoid punishment, and this holds true for both children and adults. People also lie to protect themselves or others from harm, maintain privacy, avoid embarrassment, and seek social acceptance. Low self-esteem often drives individuals to lie in order to impress or please others by telling them what they think they want to hear. Insecure teenagers, for example, may resort to lying to gain social acceptance. In such cases, it is crucial for parents to emphasize the consequences of lying to their children.

Nevertheless, some lies can have harmful consequences and cause distress. These types of lies may involve making false reports, denying events that actually occurred, or fabricating stories that have no basis in reality.

Among the most common lies that people tell are phrases like "I forgot," "I'll do it tomorrow," "I am listening," "I'm busy then," "Nice to see you," "I haven't got any change," "I've got no money," and "I got stuck in traffic." These lies often serve to avoid unwanted situations, maintain convenience, or smooth social interactions.

There are three frequently referenced categories of lies: lies of commission, lies of omission, and lies of influence (also known as character lies). People lie for various reasons, including creating excitement, appeasing others, seeking rewards, avoiding punishment, gaining attention, eliciting sympathy, and testing trust.

There are several behavioural indicators that someone may be lying, such as being vague, offering few details, repeating questions before answering them, speaking in sentence fragments, and failing to provide specific details when challenged about a story.

Lying is characterized as a false statement or presentation, known to be untrue, with the intention to deceive. Despite the moral and legal prohibitions against lying, it indicates a cognitive understanding of others' thoughts and motives, motivating individuals to lie to them.

Furthermore, individuals often tell lies to themselves. Common self-deceptive lies include believing that there is something inherently wrong with oneself, thinking that happiness will only be achieved upon attaining a specific goal, comparing oneself unfavourably to others, relying solely on positivity, and feeling inadequate. Challenging these self-deceptions and living in alignment with one's authentic self is important for personal growth and well-being.

Immanuel Kant, a German philosopher, argued that lying is always morally wrong because it contradicts the part of oneself that grants moral worth. It also deprives others of their freedom to make choices based on truthful information.

In the realm of academia, various types of academic dishonesty exist, including cheating, bribery, misrepresentation, conspiracy, fabrication, collusion, duplicate submission, and academic misconduct. These acts undermine the integrity of the educational system.

Pathological lying, although not recognized as a specific mental health disorder in the DSM-5, is a concept established in psychology. It is associated with disordered thinking patterns and beliefs, and individuals who engage in pathological lying may exhibit distorted thinking and a persistent tendency to lie.

Lying is generally considered a sin in Christianity, as stated in the commandment "thou shalt not bear false witness against thy neighbour." This can be seen in stories like the tale of Naboth in 1 Kings 21, Satya Harishchandra, and Sri Rama, where false witness leads to unjust outcomes. Lying involves giving information while knowing it to be untrue, with the intention to deceive. A lie has three key elements: it communicates information, the liar intends to deceive, and the liar believes the information to be false.

While lying is often frowned upon, it can also have negative consequences. Lying can deplete cognitive resources, increase the risk of punishment, challenge one's self-worth by undermining the perception of being a "good" person, and erode trust in society. Interestingly, the most common lies are white lies, which involve minimal dishonesty. Gray lies fall in the middle, balancing harm to others and self-preservation. On the other end, black lies intentionally harm others while protecting oneself.

Synonyms for lying include equivocating, fibbing, paltering, and prevaricating. Although these words have similar meanings, lie is the most direct term, implying outright dishonesty.

When it comes to the verb form of lie, the first example is straightforward. "To lie" means to say something that is not true, and it is a regular verb without a direct object. However, lying can have an impact on the brain. Studies published in Nature Neuroscience indicate that the amygdala, responsible for emotional responses, shows diminished activity as lying becomes more frequent. This suggests that our guilt feelings weaken and diminish over time.

Lying has a detrimental effect on relationships as it undermines trust, a fundamental pillar of any connection. Philosopher Immanuel Kant argued that if everyone lied, no one would believe anything they were told. Lying is self-defeating and toxic. Striving for truth in relationships demonstrates care for others' desires and choices.

Chronic lying can lead to an adaptation in the brain, specifically in the amygdala. This part of the brain, associated with emotions, becomes less responsive as lying becomes habitual, and making it easier to tell more audacious lies.

Compulsive lying, also known as pathological lying, mythomania, or habitual lying, describes a condition where a person tells falsehoods out of habit, sometimes without any apparent reason. The phenomenon was first described by Dr. Delbruck, a German physician, in 1891.

Children typically develop the ability to lie around the age of three. However, there are prosocial lies, which are falsehoods told for the benefit of others, and antisocial lies, which are lies told solely for personal gain. Research suggests that children develop prosocial lying abilities around the age of three.

"Ten Lies and Ten Truths" is a compilation of captivating short stories that explore foundational lies in American life. Each story delves into subjects like marriage, abortion, character, relative truth, and macro-evolution, providing thought-provoking narratives on these topics.

Lies, lies, and more lies. They permeate our lives in various forms and with different motives. It's a tangled web of deceit and deception. Let's dive into the world of lies and unravel their complexities.

In some circles, it's believed that if you disagree with someone's lifestyle, you must fear or hate them. Similarly, the notion that loving someone necessitates agreeing with everything they believe or do is also pervasive. These beliefs oversimplify the nuances of human relationships and create a black-and-white narrative.

Lies come in many shapes and sizes. From the classic scenario of denying one's involvement in breaking a vase to fabricating past experiences, lies have a way of seeping into our daily lives. Even statistics have the potential to mislead and deceive. But amidst these lies, there's a game called Two Truths and a Lie that serves as an icebreaker, revealing fascinating tidbits about us.

While lying is generally frowned upon, there are instances where it may be deemed acceptable. Lying to protect oneself or someone else from immediate danger or to safeguard someone's feelings can be justified. However, it's important to recognize that avoiding punishment often serves as the primary motivation for both children and adults when it comes to lying.

Understanding lies requires delving into the realm of deception. All lies are a form of deception, but not all deception can be labelled as lies. It's a fine line to walk and discern. Pathological lying, which typically starts in adolescence, can be associated with personality disorders like antisocial, narcissistic, and histrionic.

Detecting lies requires a keen eye and an understanding of behavioural patterns. Deviations from a person's baseline behaviour, discrepancies between words and body language, and strange emotional responses can be tell-tale signs of dishonesty.

The prefrontal cortex, the region responsible for executive control, plays a crucial role in managing lies. This part of the brain handles planning, emotional regulation, and behaviour, making it the hub of deceitful decision-making.

Pathological lying, also known as mythomania or pseudologia fantastica, is a chronic behaviour characterized by compulsive lying. These lies often serve no apparent purpose other than to paint oneself as either a hero or a victim, depending on the situation.

Lying takes its toll not only on our relationships but also on our mental and physical health. Increased heart rate, high blood pressure, and elevated stress hormone levels can be triggered by the act of lying.

Quotes about lies reveal their pervasive nature and the intricate relationship between truth and deceit. From the acknowledgment of the power of truth through lies to the understanding that lies can lead us astray, these quotes capture the essence of lies in diverse ways.

Understanding the different types of lies is key to navigating the labyrinth of deceit. Lies of denial, lies of omission, lies of fabrication, lies of minimization, and lies of exaggeration each serve their purpose in shaping deceptive narratives.

Spotting a dishonest person requires attentiveness to their speech patterns and behaviours. Absolutist statements, downplaying accomplishments, judgmental remarks, defensiveness, excessive debating, and evasive speech are all red flags of dishonesty.

The consequences of dishonesty are far-reaching, affecting an individual's reputation, relationships, and sense of self. Recommendations for good positions in society become unattainable, frequent punishment ensue, and trust is shattered, leading to isolation and shame.

Lies can be categorized into two main types: concealing and falsifying. Concealing involves withholding true information, while falsifying goes a step further by presenting false information as if it were true. Both types have their own implications and impact on truth.

In this intricate dance of truth and falsehoods, lies shape our interactions and perceptions. Understanding the motivations behind lying, detecting deception, and recognizing the consequences of dishonesty allows us to navigate this complex tapestry of lies with greater insight.

In the realm of lies, various categories and motivations come into play, shaping our understanding of truth and deception. The concept of "blue lies" emerged to describe lies told by police officers to protect their fellow law enforcement members. Within the law enforcement community, such lies were seen as morally justified when defending against external scrutiny. On the other hand, lies for personal gain, known as black lies, are universally condemned. In contrast, white lies, which are told to please others, are often perceived as harmless in everyday interactions.

Low self-esteem is identified as a primary reason for lying. People with insecurities often resort to lying in order to impress or gain approval from others. It is crucial for parents to emphasize the consequences of lying to their children. However, when it comes to the most common motives for lying, avoiding punishment emerges as the primary motivator for both children and adults. Other reasons include protecting oneself or others from harm, maintaining privacy, and avoiding embarrassment.

While some lies are told with the intention of sparing someone else's feelings or avoiding causing them pain, many lies are driven by self-preservation, protecting one's own emotions, self-esteem, or self-confidence. In some cases, individuals struggling with depression may resort to lying out of fear that their family won't understand or to avoid burdening their loved ones with their true feelings.

A lie can be defined as an intentional assertion made by a speaker with the intention to deceive, assuring the hearer of the truthfulness of a false statement. Therefore, it is deemed impossible for God, as a divine entity, to act or tell a lie. Scripture emphasizes that God is not bound by human limitations and does not engage in deceptive behaviour.

From a moral standpoint, lies are considered wrong for two main reasons. Firstly, lying corrupts the fundamental aspect of human nature, our ability to make free and rational choices. Each lie told contradicts the moral worth within us. Secondly, lies deprive others of their freedom to make rational choices by misleading them.

There are instances in various religious texts where lying is depicted as a grave transgression. For example, in the story of Ananias and Sapphira, their lie about their financial contribution resulted in severe consequences. Similarly, in the Mahabharata, Yudhishthira faced consequences for his half-truth regarding Ashwathama's death. These narratives serve as cautionary tales about the consequences of dishonesty.

Deception, as a relational transgression, can lead to feelings of betrayal and distrust between partners. Violating relational rules through deception is considered a negative breach of expectations. While some lies may have minimal impact, others can cause significant harm and distress. False reports, denials, and fabrications detached from reality fall into this category.

In contrast to the negative implications of lies, there are individuals who embody truthfulness and honesty in their lives. Harishchandra, known as Satyavadi, was revered for his commitment to truth and never speaking a lie. Yudhishthira, although an embodiment of truth, faced immense challenges and caused pain to his loved ones due to his unwavering commitment to his promise to play the game.

In the tapestry of lies, there are those who seek to deceive, while others strive for truthfulness and integrity. Understanding the complexities of lies and their motivations allows us to navigate the boundaries of truth and deception with greater insight.

Moreover, recognizing the different intentions behind deception helps us navigate the gray areas between truth and falsehood. It prompts us to question the ethical implications of our own intentions when engaging in deceptive acts and to evaluate the potential consequences of our actions on others. This deeper understanding of the intentions behind deception allows us to become more discerning individuals, capable of critically assessing the motivations behind the lies we encounter and making informed choices about our own communicative practices.

Ultimately, unravelling the diverse intentions behind deception enriches our understanding of human nature and the complex tapestry of human communication. It highlights the intricate interplay between truth and falsehood, benevolence and self-interest, and challenges us to navigate the delicate balance between protecting others and compromising authenticity. By delving into the multifaceted motivations that shape the world of deception, we gain a deeper appreciation for the complexities of human behaviour and the importance of trust, honesty, and genuine connections in our interactions with others.

Chapter 12

Deceptive lies are meticulously crafted, skilfully intertwining fragments of truth with the artistry of fiction. They come in a multitude of forms, ranging from elaborate grand narratives to cleverly constructed partial truths. The deceiver's purpose is to distort facts and manipulate information in order to serve their own agenda.

The craftsmanship of deception lies not only in the careful selection and manipulation of facts but also in the subtle art of omission. What is strategically left unsaid can be just as influential as what is revealed. This deliberate act of withholding information further enhances the deceiver's ability to shape perception and control the narrative. It creates a captivating dance between the elements of truth that are presented and the hidden aspects that remain concealed.

By delving into the captivating content of deception, we gain a deeper understanding of its construction and the profound impact it has on shaping narratives and manipulating truth. Lies are not mere fabrications; they are intricately designed constructs that aim to sway opinions, influence beliefs, and control the flow of information. The strategic blending of truth and fiction blurs the boundaries between reality and falsehood, making it challenging for others to discern the truth from the web of deceit.

Moreover, the power of deception lies not only in its immediate effects but also in its long-term consequences. When lies are perpetuated and woven into the fabric of society, they can reshape collective understanding and alter historical narratives. Deception can shape public opinion, influence decision-making processes, and even impact the course of entire nations.

Understanding the captivating content of deception allows us to be more critical consumers of information. It encourages us to question the narratives presented to us, to examine the motives behind the information we receive, and to seek multiple perspectives before forming our own judgments. By unravelling the intricacies of deceptive content, we become more adept at identifying manipulation and safeguarding ourselves against the influence of false or misleading information.

Furthermore, exploring the construction of deception raises important ethical considerations. It prompts us to reflect on the responsibility of those who engage in deceitful practices and the potential harm caused by their actions. It challenges us to consider the moral implications of manipulating truth and distorting facts for personal gain or ulterior motives.

In unravelling the captivating content of deception, we develop a heightened awareness of the power dynamics at play in communication. We recognize the importance of transparency, honesty, and integrity in fostering genuine connections and maintaining trust. By critically examining the construction and impact of deception, we equip ourselves with the tools to navigate the intricate dance between truth and falsehood, and to uphold the values that promote open and honest communication in our interactions with others.

Deception finds its place within the complex interplay of personal relationships, social interactions, and the realms of power. It infiltrates these domains, weaving its way into the intricate webs that bind individuals and societies together. Its impact is far-reaching and profound, capable of fracturing the very bonds that form the foundation of intimate connections.

In the realm of personal relationships, deception poses a formidable threat to trust. When lies are introduced into the dynamics of love, friendship, and family, they erode the bedrock of honesty and authenticity. Deception undermines the fundamental trust that sustains these relationships, creating fissures that can be challenging to repair. The betrayal of trust leaves individuals grappling with feelings of hurt, confusion, and disillusionment.

In social dynamics, deception poses a constant challenge to authenticity. As individuals navigate the intricacies of social interactions, there is often a delicate balance between revealing one's true self and presenting a carefully constructed façade. Deception blurs the lines between genuine connection and calculated pretence. It fosters an environment where individuals may feel pressured to project an image that conforms to societal expectations or personal agendas, rather than embracing their true identities. This pervasive presence of deception within social contexts hinders the development of deep and meaningful connections based on mutual trust and understanding.

In the corridors of power, deception emerges as a potent weapon with far-reaching consequences. In the realm of politics and business, lies are strategically employed to shape public opinion, influence decision-making processes, and consolidate power. Political deception and manipulation of information have the potential to sway the collective beliefs and actions of entire societies. In the world of business, deceptive practices can lead to unfair advantages, undermine competition, and harm stakeholders. Deception within these contexts has profound implications for individuals, communities, and even nations, as it shapes the trajectory of policies, institutions, and the distribution of resources.

By understanding the contextual dimensions of deception, we gain a comprehensive perspective on its implications and the dynamics it engenders. Recognizing the presence of deception within personal relationships alerts us to the importance of cultivating trust, honesty, and open communication. In social dynamics, understanding the pervasive nature of deception urges us to foster environments that encourage authenticity and genuine connections. Moreover, comprehending the role of deception in politics and business prompts us to be critical consumers of information, to seek transparency and accountability, and to advocate for ethical practices.

We can better prepare ourselves to navigate these intricate webs of deception by shedding light on the contextual aspects of deception.

We have the capacity to build strong and trustworthy relationships, make good choices, and

Contribute to the development of a more open and authentic society.

The consequences of deception linger long after the lies have been told, echoing through the realm of trust. Like a ripple in a pond, the aftermath of deceit tarnishes reputations, fractures relationships, and plants seeds of doubt and suspicion. It erodes the very foundations on which human connections are built, leaving a trail of destruction that affects both the deceiver and the deceived.

When trust is shattered, it takes immense effort to rebuild. Deception undermines the faith we place in others, leaving us questioning the authenticity of their words and actions. Reputations, carefully cultivated over time, can be irreparably damaged by the revelation of deceit. The deceiver becomes a figure of scepticism, their motives and intentions cast into doubt.

On the interpersonal level, deception fractures relationships. The revelation of lies can cause immense pain and betrayal, leading to a breakdown in communication and emotional distance. The deceived may struggle with feelings of anger, hurt, and a loss of faith in their ability to discern truth from falsehood. Trust, once broken, becomes fragile, and repairing the bond between individuals becomes an arduous journey.

Beyond the personal realm, deception's impact extends to society as a whole. When deceit permeates the collective consciousness, it erodes the fabric of social cohesion. Suspicion and cynicism replace trust and cooperation. The seeds of doubt sow division, making it difficult for communities to come together and address common challenges. Trust in institutions, whether they are governmental, corporate, or societal, can be irreversibly damaged, resulting in a breakdown of social order and stability.

The consequences of deception are profound and far-reaching, shaping not only personal destinies but also the trajectory of societies. Individuals and communities are left grappling with the aftermath, struggling to rebuild trust and restore faith in their fellow human beings. The power of deception lies not only in the immediate act of lying but also in its lasting impact, which reverberates through the intricate networks of human connections.

By delving into the effects of deception, we come to recognize the immense responsibility that lies in our hands. We must strive for integrity, transparency, and honesty in our own actions and interactions. Rebuilding trust requires acts of vulnerability, empathy, and genuine remorse. Collectively, we must cultivate a culture that values truth and upholds the principles of integrity.

Understanding the consequences of deception prompts us to reflect on our own behaviour and to be discerning consumers of information. It compels us to demand transparency and accountability from those in positions of power. By actively working to restore trust and promote honesty, we contribute to the healing of fractured relationships and the revitalization of social bonds.

The aftermath of deception serves as a stark reminder of the profound impact that lies can have on individuals and societies. It calls us to be vigilant, compassionate, and committed to the restoration of trust. Only by acknowledging the far-reaching effects of deception can we begin to rebuild what has been broken and forge a path towards a more honest and interconnected world.

Deception, woven intricately into the very fabric of our existence, serves as a mirror that reflects the depths of our desires, fears, and vulnerabilities. It is a phenomenon that challenges the very notions of morality and integrity, forcing us to confront our own ethical boundaries. In this process, deception becomes more than just a tool for manipulation; it becomes a catalyst for self-exploration, inviting us to embark on a profound journey of questioning, reflection, and self-understanding.

Through the lens of deception, we gain insights into the intricate workings of human nature. It exposes our innate desires for self-preservation, recognition, and power, as well as our fears of rejection, failure, and vulnerability. By observing how lies are crafted and employed, we gain a deeper understanding of the motivations that drive human behaviour. Deception serves as a pathway to unravel the complexities of our desires, shedding light on the intricate tapestry of human emotions and motivations.

Furthermore, deception forces us to examine the mechanisms of communication that underlie our interactions with others. It reveals the delicate balance between what we choose to reveal and what we keep hidden, the subtle nuances of verbal and nonverbal cues, and the power dynamics at play in our relationships. By dissecting the intricacies of deception, we develop a heightened awareness of the ways in which communication can be manipulated and distorted.

Engaging with the concept of deception propels us towards introspection and self-discovery. It urges us to question our own capacity for honesty and integrity, to confront the instances in which we may have been complicit in deceiving others or even ourselves. By delving into the complexities of deception, we are confronted with the uncomfortable truth that we, too, possess the potential for dishonesty.

In this journey of self-exploration, we are compelled to confront our own vulnerabilities and insecurities. Deception exposes the fragility of our self-image and the façades we construct to protect ourselves. It invites us to examine the ways in which we use deception as a shield, a defence mechanism against judgment and rejection. By unravelling the complexities of deception, we confront our own vulnerabilities and embark on a path of growth and authenticity.

Ultimately, the exploration of deception serves as a catalyst for personal and interpersonal growth. It challenges us to cultivate a deeper sense of self-awareness, empathy, and compassion. By recognizing the motivations behind deception, we can develop a greater understanding and acceptance of the complexities inherent in human nature. We become more attuned to the power dynamics at play in our relationships, fostering empathy and connection. Through this process, we move closer to a more authentic and genuine way of being.

In unravelling the multifaceted nature of deception, we are confronted with profound questions about our own moral compass, the nature of truth, and the ways in which we navigate the complex web of human communication. It is a journey that demands introspection, self-reflection, and a willingness to confront our own vulnerabilities. By embracing this journey, we gain a deeper understanding of ourselves, our relationships, and the world around us.

Chapter 13

Deception, characterized by its intricate interplay of intentions, content, and context, continues to captivate and mystify us as a powerful force in human interactions. To navigate this complex terrain, it is essential to grasp the diverse dimensions of deception, enabling us to navigate its treacherous waters with heightened awareness and discernment. As we embark on this quest to unravel the intricacies of deception, we are called upon to cultivate a society founded on trust, transparency, and empathy, where truth can emerge from the shadows.

To effectively navigate the realm of deception, we must first acknowledge the diverse intentions that drive individuals to engage in deceptive practices. By recognizing that motives can range from benevolence to self-interest, we gain insight into the complex tapestry of human desires and intentions. Armed with this understanding, we can approach deceptive situations with a discerning eye, evaluating the underlying motives and potential consequences.

The content of deception, intricately crafted to manipulate perceptions, plays a central role in the dance of deception. Whether through the artful blend of truth and fiction or the deliberate omission of crucial information, deceivers create a narrative that serves their purpose. By exploring the captivating content of deception, we gain a deeper understanding of the manipulative techniques employed and the delicate balance between revelation and concealment. This knowledge empowers us to critically analyse information presented to us, ensuring that we do not fall prey to deceitful tactics.

Context, another crucial element in the realm of deception, shapes the dynamics of deceit in various domains of human interaction. From personal relationships to social settings and positions of power, the contextual backdrop influences the strategies employed and the impact of deception. By recognizing the contextual dimensions of deception, we can better comprehend its intricacies and navigate the complex web of social interactions with greater discernment and caution.

In our quest for truth amidst the shadows of deception, we must remain vigilant and committed to fostering a society built on trust, transparency, and empathy. By upholding these values, we create an environment where deception is less likely to thrive. Trust becomes the bedrock upon which genuine connections and authentic relationships are built, allowing us to navigate the complexities of human interaction with integrity and compassion.

By delving into the multifaceted nature of deception, we embark on a journey of self-discovery and a deeper understanding of the world we inhabit. Unveiling the complexities of deception serves as a mirror that reflects our own vulnerabilities, fears, and desires. It challenges us to examine our own roles in perpetuating or combatting deception and invites us to strive for authenticity in our interactions.

Ultimately, by unravelling the intricacies of deception, we forge a path towards genuine connections and authentic relationships. We become more attuned to the subtleties of human communication, cultivating empathy and understanding. Through this journey, we not only gain insight into ourselves but also contribute to the creation of a society rooted in truth, transparency, and compassion.

Chapter 14

The relationship between technologies and lies is a complex and ever-evolving one, encompassing both enabling and exposing aspects. Technologies have the potential to facilitate the spread of deception, create new forms of deceit, and also provide tools for detecting and uncovering lies.

One way in which technologies enable lies is through social media platforms. These platforms have become breeding grounds for misinformation, disinformation, and propaganda. They allow for the rapid dissemination of false narratives, as well as the creation of fake profiles, posts, and reviews. The ease of sharing and the wide reach of social media contribute to the amplification of deceptive content, posing challenges for individuals and societies to discern truth from falsehood.

Artificial intelligence (AI) and deep learning technologies present another avenue for enabling deception. Through the creation of deep fakes, AI algorithms can generate realistic but fake images, videos, and audio that can be used to impersonate, manipulate, or defame individuals or groups. This technology blurs the line between reality and fiction, making it increasingly difficult to distinguish between genuine and manipulated media.

Encryption and anonymization tools, while valuable for protecting privacy and security, can also enable deception. These technologies allow individuals to hide their identities and activities online, making it challenging to hold them accountable for their actions. In some cases, this anonymity can be exploited to engage in deceptive practices, such as spreading false information or engaging in illegal activities.

On the other hand, technologies can also play a role in exposing lies and promoting transparency. Lie detection technologies, such as polygraph tests, brain scans, eye tracking, voice analysis, and facial recognition, provide methods for measuring physiological or behavioural cues of deception. These tools can be used in various contexts, such as criminal investigations or employment screenings, to uncover dishonesty.

Digital forensics and fact-checking tools are instrumental in verifying the authenticity and accuracy of digital data. Through the analysis of images, videos, audio, text, or metadata, these technologies can help identify manipulated or misleading information. They provide a means to counteract deception by providing evidence-based assessments of the veracity of claims or sources.

Block chain and biometric technologies offer secure and transparent ways to store and verify identity and transactions. By leveraging the immutability and decentralization of block chain, and the uniqueness of biometric data, these technologies mitigate the risk of fraud and corruption. They provide mechanisms to validate the integrity of information and transactions, reducing the potential for deception.

However, technologies also introduce new forms and challenges of deception. Cyber-attacks and hacking pose significant risks to digital systems and data. These attacks can compromise the integrity and confidentiality of information, resulting in data breaches, identity theft, ransom ware, or sabotage. The deceptive tactics employed in cyber-attacks create challenges for organizations and individuals to protect themselves and their sensitive information.

Online deception and fraud have become prevalent in the digital age. Individuals with malicious intent exploit the trust and vulnerability of online users through practices such as phishing, scamming, cat fishing, or cyber bullying. These forms of deception leverage the anonymity and interconnectedness of the online world, necessitating vigilance and awareness among internet users.

Moreover, the pervasive use of technology and the constant access to digital devices have given rise to concerns about digital addiction and distraction. Excessive reliance on technology can impact mental health and well-being, leading to reduced attention spans, impaired memory, increased stress, and decreased social skills. These effects can indirectly contribute to the spread and acceptance of deceptive information as individuals become more susceptible to manipulation.

The connection between technologies and lies is complex and evolving. Technology has the ability to enable and reveal lies, as well as produce new difficulties and types of deception. People, societies, and policymakers must negotiate this complicated environment with a critical perspective while fostering transparency, accountability, and openness as technology develops.

Chapter 15

Lies are prevalent in society, and people often construct them to manipulate others, protect themselves, or achieve their goals. The act of lying involves intentionally distorting the truth, which can have significant implications for justice, relationships, and societal well-being. In this analysis, we will explore the prevalence of lies, the motivations behind constructing them, and their impact on truth and justice through case studies.

1. Prevalence of Lies:

Lies can be found in various aspects of life, from personal interactions to professional settings. People may lie to avoid punishment, gain personal advantages, or maintain a positive self-image. In relationships, lies can be used to conceal infidelity, hide personal flaws, or manipulate emotions. In business, lies may be employed to deceive customers, competitors, or stakeholders. Lies can also permeate the political sphere, where politicians may make false promises or spread misinformation to manipulate public opinion.

2. Motivations for Constructing Lies:

People construct lies for a range of reasons. Self-preservation is a common motive, where individuals lie to avoid negative consequences or protect their reputation. Self-interest can drive individuals to lie to achieve personal gain, whether it is financial, professional, or social advantages. In some cases, lies may be born out of a desire to control or manipulate others. Additionally, lies can emerge from fear, shame, or the desire to avoid conflict or hurt feelings.

3. Distorting Truth and Justice:

Lies can have a detrimental impact on truth and justice, undermining the very foundations of a fair and equitable society. When lies are introduced into legal proceedings, they can result in wrongful convictions, impede the discovery of evidence, or manipulate the perception of guilt or innocence. False testimonies, perjury, or the suppression of evidence can distort the truth, leading to unjust outcomes and a loss of faith in the justice system.

Case Studies:

a. The Enron Scandal: In the early 2000s, Enron, an American energy company, collapsed due to accounting fraud and widespread deception. Executives engaged in manipulating financial statements, hiding debts, and inflating profits to deceive investors and maintain the appearance of success. The lies and distortions of truth eventually led to the downfall of the company and impacted the lives of thousands of employees and shareholders.

B. Lance Armstrong Doping Scandal: Lance Armstrong, a renowned cyclist, achieved numerous victories and titles, while vehemently denying accusations of using performance-enhancing drugs. However, he later confessed to years of doping and deceiving the public, tarnishing his legacy and causing significant damage to the sport's reputation. Armstrong's lies distorted the truth and compromised the fairness and integrity of competitive cycling.

c. Central Park Five: In 1989, five teenagers were wrongfully convicted of a brutal assault in New York City's Central Park. The case was marred by coerced confessions, false testimonies, and media manipulation, leading to the wrongful incarceration of innocent individuals. The lies and distortions of truth resulted in a grave miscarriage of justice, impacting the lives of the wrongfully accused and highlighting systemic issues within the criminal justice system.

These case studies illustrate how lies and distortions of truth can have far-reaching consequences, not only for individuals directly involved but also for wider societal trust and justice. They demonstrate the need for vigilance, transparency, and a commitment to uncovering the truth, even in the face of deception.

Lies are pervasive in many aspects of life, and the way they are constructed can affect what is true and what is just. In order to fight deception and promote fairness and honesty, it is essential to comprehend the causes of falsehoods and the effects they have on people and society. Through case study analysis, we learn about the serious repercussions of lying and the significance of establishing a culture that values honesty, transparency, and responsibility.

Chapter 16

Lies and misleading information are unfortunately prevalent in the world of business and sales. Corporations and individuals often resort to deceptive tactics to gain a competitive edge, maximize profits, or protect their reputation. This unethical behaviour not only undermines trust between businesses and consumers but also erodes the integrity of the marketplace. In this discussion, we will explore the reasons behind the prevalence of lies and misleading information in business and sales, the techniques employed the consequences for both stakeholders and society, and the ethical and legal implications and solutions.

1. Motivations for Deception:

In the business world, the motivations behind lies and misleading information can be diverse. Companies may engage in false advertising to create a favourable image of their products or services, leading to increased sales. Misrepresenting product features, benefits, or performance can mislead consumers into making uninformed purchasing decisions. Businesses may also withhold or manipulate information about potential risks or side effects to promote their offerings.

The pursuit of profit often drives corporations to prioritize short-term gains over long-term customer satisfaction. In a competitive environment, companies may resort to dishonest practices to outdo their rivals or secure market share. Additionally, the pressure to meet financial targets and shareholder expectations can incentivize businesses to manipulate financial statements or provide false information to investors.

Individuals may also engage in deception for personal or professional reasons. Salespeople may lie about their qualifications, achievements, or commissions to impress their employers or customers. Customers may lie about their needs, preferences, or budgets to negotiate better deals or obtain refunds. Employees may lie about their performance, attendance, or expenses to avoid criticism or obtain rewards.

2. Techniques Employed:

Businesses employ various techniques to deceive consumers and stakeholders. Some common tactics include:

- False or exaggerated claims: Companies may make claims about their products or services that are not supported by evidence or are exaggerated to create a perception of superiority or unique benefits. For example, in 2015, Volkswagen admitted that it had installed software in millions of diesel vehicles that cheated emissions tests and made them appear more environmentally friendly than they were.

- Hidden fees or terms: Businesses may intentionally conceal additional costs, fees, or unfavourable terms in contracts or agreements, leading to unexpected charges or disadvantages for consumers. For example, in 2016, Wells Fargo agreed to pay $185 million in fines for opening millions of unauthorized accounts for customers and charging those fees without their consent.

- Manipulative marketing: Techniques like bait-and-switch, where a company advertises a product at a low price but then pushes customers to purchase a more expensive alternative, or aggressive upselling can manipulate consumer choices. For example, in 2017, Amazon was fined $1.1 million by Canada's Competition Bureau for using misleading price comparisons that made customers believe they were getting bigger discounts than they actually were.

- Fake reviews and testimonials: Companies may generate false positive reviews or testimonials to enhance their reputation or create a perception of widespread customer satisfaction. For example, in 2019, Facebook removed hundreds of accounts that were involved in coordinated campaigns to post fake reviews for products sold on Amazon.

3. Consequences for Stakeholders and Society:

The prevalence of lies and misleading information in business and sales has significant consequences:

- Consumer harm: Consumers who fall victim to deceptive practices may experience financial loss, health risks, or disappointment with the products or services they purchased. This erodes trust and damages the relationship between businesses and consumers.

- Reputation damage: Companies that engage in dishonest practices risk damaging their reputation and losing the trust of their customers. Negative publicity, boycotts, or legal actions can result from such behaviour, leading to financial and reputational losses.

- Market distortion: When businesses rely on lies and misleading information, it distorts the competitive landscape. Honest businesses may struggle to compete, and consumers may find it challenging to make informed choices, leading to market inefficiencies.

- Legal and regulatory repercussions: Engaging in deceptive practices can result in legal consequences, such as lawsuits, fines, or regulatory intervention. Authorities and consumer protection agencies often take action against businesses that deceive consumers.

4. Ethical and Legal Implications and Solutions:

Lies and misleading information in business and sales raise ethical and legal issues that require attention and action from various stakeholders.

- Ethical principles and values: Businesses should adhere to ethical principles and values that guide their conduct, such as honesty, integrity, fairness, transparency, accountability, etc. These principles and values should be reflected in their policies, practices, and culture, and communicated to their employees, customers, and partners.

- Laws and regulations:

Businesses should comply with the laws and regulations that prohibit or penalize deceptive practices, such as consumer protection laws, trade practices laws, advertising standards, etc.

These laws and regulations should be enforced by authorities and consumer protection agencies to protect the rights and interests of consumers and stakeholders.

- Strategies and solutions:

Consumers, businesses, and regulators can adopt various strategies and solutions to prevent

Or reduce lies and misleading information in business and sales, such as:

- Educating consumers about their rights and responsibilities, and providing them with information and resources to verify and report deceptive practices.

- Verifying information from multiple sources, and seeking independent opinions or advice before making purchasing decisions.

- Reporting or exposing deceptive practices, and seeking legal remedies or compensation when harmed by deception.

- Enforcing ethical codes and standards, and imposing sanctions or penalties for violating them.

- Promoting transparency and accountability, and rewarding honesty and integrity.

Section 1: The Ethical Perspective

In the world of business and sales, lies and misleading information have become all too common. However, from an ethical standpoint, these practices are highly questionable and raise significant concerns. In this section, we will delve into the ethical dimensions of lies and misleading information in business and sales, emphasizing the importance of trust, long-term sustainability, and alternative strategies for success.

At the core of ethical business practices lies the principle of trust. Trust forms the foundation of successful relationships between businesses and consumers, as well as between businesses and stakeholders. When lies and misleading information enter the picture, this foundation crumbles, leading to a breakdown in trust and eroding the very essence of a healthy business ecosystem.

Lies and misleading information in business and sales are fundamentally unethical as they violate the principles of honesty, transparency, and fairness. Businesses have a moral responsibility to provide accurate information about their products, services, and operations. Misrepresenting facts, making false claims, or withholding crucial information not only undermines the trust of consumers but also breaches their right to make informed choices.

Moreover, lies and misleading information are not only ethically questionable but also short-sighted and counterproductive. While these practices may provide temporary benefits or advantages, they come at the cost of long-term risks and costs. Businesses that engage in deceptive practices expose themselves to reputational damage, legal liabilities, and a loss of customer satisfaction and loyalty.

Lies and deceptions, those crafty chameleons of truth, slither their way into various nooks and crannies of life, finding fertile ground especially within the public and business realms, not only in India but across the globe. In the realm of politics, where power and influence collide, politicians master the art of deception, weaving intricate webs of lies to sway public opinion, safeguard their interests, and manipulate the course of democracy. A damning report by the Association for Democratic Reforms (ADR) exposed a startling reality in 2019, revealing that 43% of newly elected members of parliament in India carried pending criminal cases many of whom conveniently concealed or distorted information about their tarnished records in their affidavits.

The business and sales domain, driven by ambition and profit, presents a fertile breeding ground for deception. Entrepreneurs and salespeople adeptly wield falsehoods to entice customers, secure funding, gain a competitive edge, evade legal consequences, or even circumvent regulatory compliance. The infamous Punjab National Bank (PNB) fraud case in 2018 sent shockwaves through the nation as billionaire jeweller Nirav Modi, in cahoots with his associates, orchestrated a colossal scam, siphoning off over US$2 billion by employing counterfeit letters of undertaking and colluding with bank officials.

Even the pursuit of knowledge and truth is not immune to the allure of deception. Students and researchers, driven by academic pressures or the pursuit of fame, resort to dishonest tactics, including plagiarism, falsified data, or biased reporting, in their quest for success and recognition. In India, a 2019 study conducted by Turnitin, a leading plagiarism detection service, revealed an alarming statistic: among 15 countries surveyed, India ranked the highest in academic plagiarism, with a staggering 62% of undergraduate papers containing unoriginal content.

In the realm of law and justice, where the scales of truth must be meticulously balanced, even the purveyors of justice can be seduced by deceit. Lawyers and witnesses, driven by the desire to secure favourable outcomes, resort to fabricating evidence, concealing truths, or manipulating testimonies. The consequences are dire, with the National Judicial Data Grid (NJDG) reporting a staggering backlog of over 3.5 crore pending cases in Indian courts in 2019, many of which faced delays and complications due to false or manufactured evidence.

While lies and deceptions may seem to have infiltrated every corner of public and business life in India, it is crucial to note that not every individual within these domains is consumed by falsehoods. The frequency and severity of deception vary depending on contextual factors, individual motivations, and ethical inclinations. Furthermore, the implications of lying and deceiving extend beyond personal morality, often encroaching upon the ethical and legal boundaries that shape our society.

To combat this pervasive challenge, a collective effort is required. Strengthening regulations, promoting transparency, and cultivating a culture of integrity and accountability can help re-establish trust within these domains. Equipping individuals with the knowledge and tools to detect and confront deception empowers them to navigate these treacherous waters and safeguards the foundation of an honest and just society.

In the grand tapestry of life, where truth and lies intertwine, the battle against deception is an on-going struggle. By shining a light on the areas where lies and deceptions commonly occur, we uncover the complex dynamics that perpetuate these practices. With unwavering determination, ethical reflection, and stringent measures, we can work towards a future where truth triumphs over deceit, fostering an environment that values integrity, transparency, and the pursuit of a more honest and just society.

Reputation is a vital asset for any business, and once tarnished, it is challenging to rebuild. Consumers today have access to a plethora of information and platforms to share their experiences and opinions. Word spreads quickly, and businesses caught in lies and misleading practices can face severe backlash, leading to significant financial and reputational losses. The consequences can extend beyond individual businesses and impact entire industries, eroding public trust and confidence.

Lies and misleading information have far-reaching consequences for society, eroding ethical standards, fair competition, and fostering scepticism. These practices not only harm individual consumers but also undermine the overall well-being of communities. While lies and deceptions are prevalent in various aspects of life, it is essential to recognize that not everyone engages in such behaviour to the same extent. Motivations, contexts, and individual differences contribute to the frequency and severity of deception in different domains. The prevalence of lies and deceptions also raises ethical and legal concerns, necessitating efforts to promote honesty, transparency, and accountability in our interactions.

1. Personal relationships: In personal relationships, individuals may resort to lies or deceptions to manage conflicts, protect the feelings of loved ones, maintain trust, conceal secrets, impress others, or manipulate situations. These deceptive acts can undermine trust and intimacy, leading to strained relationships and emotional harm. Building open and honest communication is crucial for fostering healthy personal relationships based on trust and respect.

2. Politics: Lies and deceptions are unfortunately commonplace in politics. Politicians may use falsehoods to sway public opinion, win elections, advance their agendas, or cover up scandals. This manipulation of information erodes trust in political systems and

hinders the ability of citizens to make informed decisions. Maintaining transparency, accountability, and promoting fact-checking and media literacy are essential for ensuring the integrity of democratic processes.

3. Business and sales: Lies and misleading information in business and sales can have severe consequences. Companies or salespeople may engage in deceptive practices to boost sales, attract investments, gain a competitive edge, evade legal liabilities, or comply with regulations. These actions harm consumers, erode trust in businesses, and can result in financial losses or health risks. Ethical business practices, consumer protection regulations, and responsible marketing strategies are essential for maintaining a fair and trustworthy marketplace.

4. Education and research: Lies and deceptions in education and research undermine the pursuit of knowledge and the integrity of academic institutions. Students and researchers may be tempted to fabricate or manipulate data, plagiarize work, or misrepresent findings to achieve academic success, secure funding, or support their hypotheses. Such dishonesty erodes the credibility of educational and research institutions and hampers scientific progress. Upholding academic integrity, promoting ethical research practices, and nurturing a culture of honesty and intellectual rigor are crucial for the advancement of knowledge.

5. Law and justice: Lies and deceptions in the legal system can compromise the fairness and integrity of the justice system. Lawyers may engage in deceitful tactics to win cases, protect clients, or manipulate evidence, while witnesses may provide false testimonies to influence the outcome of trials. These actions obstruct justice, jeopardize the rights of individuals, and erode public trust in the legal system. Upholding professional ethics, ensuring fair trial procedures, and promoting truth-seeking practices are vital for maintaining the integrity of the justice system.

In each of these areas, lies and deceptions have significant implications and consequences. They erode trust, hinder progress, and can result in financial, emotional, or legal harm to individuals and society as a whole. It is crucial for individuals, institutions, and societies to prioritize ethical conduct, transparency, and accountability to combat the prevalence of lies and deceptions. Promoting values such as honesty, integrity, and ethical decision-making is essential for creating a culture that upholds the importance of truth and justice.

Critics may argue that lies and misleading information are necessary in the highly competitive business landscape, where businesses vie for attention, market share, and profitability. However, this perspective fails to acknowledge the alternative strategies for success that are both ethical and effective.

Providing quality products or services lies at the heart of ethical business practices. By prioritizing customer satisfaction, businesses can build a loyal customer base and establish a positive reputation. By focusing on delivering value and meeting customer needs, businesses can create long-term relationships that are based on trust and mutual benefit.

Transparency is another key principle that businesses should uphold. Clear and accurate communication with consumers, stakeholders, and the public ensures that everyone involved has access to the necessary information to make informed decisions. Openness and honesty foster trust, enhance credibility, and contribute to a positive business environment.

Innovation and excellence are also crucial components of ethical business practices. By continually striving to improve products, services, and processes, businesses can remain competitive without resorting to lies or misleading information. Investing in research and development, embracing sustainable practices, and promoting corporate social responsibility are ways businesses can demonstrate their commitment to ethical conduct and societal well-being.

The world of business and sales is not a place for lies and false information. These actions are unethical because they go against the values of justice, transparency, and trust. They have negative effects on society as a whole in addition to the business-consumer interaction. Adopting alternate approaches to success, such as emphasising transparency, innovation, and high-quality standards, is not only morally right but also advantageous in the long run. Businesses may help create a free and honest market that looks out for the interests of all interested parties by respecting ethical standards.

This section delves deeper into the consequences that result from lies and misleading information in business and sales. It highlights the detrimental effects on consumers and businesses, shedding light on the importance of ethical conduct and the maintenance of a healthy marketplace.

One of the most significant consequences of lies and misleading information is the negative impact on consumers. When consumers are deceived, they may suffer financial loss and make purchases based on false claims or inaccurate information. For example, a consumer who buys a product that does not deliver on its promised features or benefits may experience financial hardship. This can lead to a loss of trust in businesses and scepticism towards future purchases.

Furthermore, lies and misleading information can have severe implications for consumer health and safety. In industries such as pharmaceuticals or food production, inaccurate claims or hidden risks can jeopardize the well-being of consumers. For instance, if a company misrepresents the side effects or efficacy of a medication, individuals may unknowingly put their health at risk. Such deceptive practices not only harm consumers but also erode confidence in the industry as a whole.

Another significant consequence lies in the reputational damage suffered by businesses engaged in deceptive practices. Negative publicity can spread rapidly in today's interconnected world, fuelled by social media and online platforms. Consumers who have been deceived often share their experiences, warning others and tarnishing the reputation of the business involved. This can result in a significant loss of customer trust, decreased sales, and diminished brand loyalty.

In addition to the impact on consumers, businesses that engage in lies and misleading information face legal repercussions. Misrepresentation of products or services can lead to legal actions, such as lawsuits for false advertising or fraud. Companies found guilty of deceptive practices may face substantial fines and penalties, which can have severe financial implications. Legal battles also consume valuable resources and divert attention from core business operations.

Reputational damage and legal repercussions can have long-lasting effects on a company's bottom line. Businesses that lose the trust of their customers may struggle to regain their market position and recover from the damage caused by deceptive practices. This can result in decreased sales, loss of market share, and a decline in overall profitability. Furthermore, the negative publicity associated with lies and misleading information can harm relationships with suppliers, partners, and investors, further impacting the company's ability to operate successfully.

Moreover, the loss of customer loyalty is a significant consequence for businesses. When consumers discover they have been deceived, they often feel betrayed and develop a sense of distrust towards the company. They are less likely to repeat purchases, recommend the brand to others, or engage in positive word-of-mouth. This loss of loyalty can be challenging to overcome, as building trust takes time and consistent ethical behaviour.

By outlining these consequences, it becomes evident that lies and misleading information in business and sales have far-reaching effects. The negative impact on consumers' finances, health, and confidence, coupled with the reputational damage and legal repercussions faced by businesses, underscores the significance of ethical conduct.

Maintaining a healthy marketplace requires businesses to prioritize transparency, honesty, and fairness in their practices. By delivering accurate information, ensuring the safety and quality of products and services, and acting in the best interests of consumers, businesses can foster trust and build lasting relationships. Ethical conduct not only benefits consumers but also provides long-term sustainability for businesses, promoting a fair and trustworthy marketplace that benefits all stakeholders involved.

To provide a comprehensive understanding of the issue at hand, it is essential to examine real-life case studies that highlight the prevalence and consequences of lies and misleading information in business and sales. These examples serve as poignant illustrations of the harm caused to consumers, businesses, and society as a whole. By analysing cases involving false advertising, hidden fees, and manipulative marketing tactics, we gain insight into the deceptive practices that have deceived and harmed unsuspecting customers.

One notable case that exemplifies the consequences of false advertising is the Volkswagen emissions scandal. In 2015, it was revealed that Volkswagen had equipped its diesel vehicles with software designed to manipulate emissions tests, providing false data on the vehicles' environmental impact. This deliberate deception not only misled consumers who believed they were purchasing environmentally friendly cars but also had significant environmental consequences. The scandal led to billions of dollars in fines and settlements for Volkswagen, severely damaging the company's reputation and resulting in a loss of consumer trust.

Another case that highlights the harm caused by lies and misleading information is the Wells Fargo account fraud scandal. In 2016, it was discovered that Wells Fargo employees had opened millions of unauthorized bank accounts on behalf of customers without their consent. The employees engaged in this unethical practice to meet aggressive sales targets and earn incentives. As a result, customers suffered financial harm, including unauthorized fees, damaged credit scores, and reputational damage. Wells Fargo faced legal consequences, including substantial fines and the resignation of its CEO. The incident underscored the need for stricter regulations and ethical standards in the banking industry to prevent such deceptive practices.

Hidden fees are another common form of misleading information that can harm consumers. An example of this is the case of mobile phone service providers. Many customers have experienced surprise charges and hidden fees in their monthly bills, such as administrative fees, activation fees, or early termination fees. These undisclosed charges can significantly impact consumers' finances and create a sense of distrust towards the company. The Federal Communications Commission (FCC) has taken action to address this issue by implementing regulations that require service providers to disclose all fees and charges clearly.

Manipulative marketing tactics are also prevalent in the business world, with the intention of persuading consumers to make purchasing decisions based on misleading information. One well-known example is the tobacco industry's history of deceptive marketing. For decades, tobacco companies downplayed the health risks associated with smoking, targeted youth through advertising, and manipulated scientific research to create doubt about the harms of tobacco. These tactics not only misled consumers about the dangers of smoking but also contributed to the devastating health consequences and societal costs associated with tobacco-related illnesses. Stricter regulations, public awareness campaigns, and legal actions have been instrumental in curbing these deceptive practices and holding tobacco companies accountable.

These case studies serve as powerful reminders of the prevalence and consequences of lies and misleading information in business and sales. They demonstrate the tangible harm caused to consumers who place their trust in companies and rely on accurate information to make informed decisions. The financial, reputational, and health consequences suffered by individuals and society at large underscore the urgent need for stricter regulations and ethical standards to combat these unethical practices.

In response to such cases, regulatory bodies and consumer advocacy groups have been working to enhance consumer protection laws and promote transparency in business practices. Stricter regulations on advertising, disclosure requirements, and penalties for deceptive practices are necessary to hold businesses accountable and deter future misconduct. Moreover, fostering a culture of ethical behaviour and corporate social responsibility can help businesses prioritize the well-being of consumers and maintain trust in the marketplace.

Ultimately, by examining these case studies and understanding the far-reaching implications of lies and misleading information, we reinforce the importance of ethical conduct, transparency, and consumer empowerment. It is crucial for businesses to prioritize the truth, act responsibly, and uphold the trust placed in them by consumers. Equally important is the role of consumers in staying informed, demanding transparency, and supporting ethical businesses. By working together, we can create a business environment that fosters honesty, fairness, and the well-being of all stakeholders involved.

In light of the negative consequences associated with lies and misleading information in business and sales, it is crucial to explore alternative strategies that businesses can adopt to achieve success and competitiveness while upholding ethical standards. By shifting their focus towards sustainable practices and fostering positive relationships with customers and stakeholders, businesses can thrive without resorting to deceptive tactics.

One key strategy for businesses is to prioritize the delivery of quality products or services. By investing in research and development, quality control processes, and continuous improvement, businesses can ensure that their offerings meet or exceed customer expectations.

Providing reliable, durable, and functional products or services not only enhances customer satisfaction but also builds a reputation for trust and reliability. Satisfied customers are more likely to become loyal advocates, referring others and contributing to long-term success.

Delivering value and satisfaction is another important aspect that businesses should prioritize. This involves offering competitive pricing, transparent pricing structures, and fair terms and conditions. By clearly communicating the value proposition of their products or services, businesses can help customers make informed decisions and feel confident about their purchases. This approach establishes a foundation of trust and fosters positive customer experiences, leading to customer loyalty and repeat business.

Building customer loyalty and trust is paramount in cultivating long-term relationships. This can be achieved through open and honest communication, responsive customer service, and personalized experiences. By listening to customer feedback, addressing concerns, and resolving issues promptly and effectively, businesses can demonstrate their commitment to customer satisfaction. Moreover, being transparent about business practices, policies, and any changes that may impact customers further strengthens trust and fosters a sense of loyalty.

Fostering innovation and excellence is another avenue for businesses to differentiate themselves in the marketplace. By investing in research and development, embracing new technologies, and staying ahead of industry trends, businesses can continuously improve their offerings and stay competitive. Genuine innovation allows businesses to provide unique and valuable solutions to customers, setting them apart from competitors. Furthermore, a commitment to excellence in all aspects of operations, including customer service, manufacturing processes, and supply chain management, contributes to a positive brand image and customer perception.

By adopting these alternative strategies, businesses can cultivate long-term success while upholding ethical conduct and avoiding the pitfalls associated with lies and misleading information. Embracing these principles not only benefits businesses themselves but also contributes to the overall health and trustworthiness of the marketplace.

Several successful companies serve as prime examples of how ethical business practices can lead to sustainable success. For instance, Patagonia, an outdoor clothing and gear retailer, has built a reputation for its commitment to environmental sustainability and social responsibility. The company transparently communicates its efforts to minimize its environmental impact and supports various environmental initiatives. By aligning their business values with customer values, Patagonia has established a loyal customer base that appreciates the brand's authenticity and commitment to making a positive impact.

Another example is TOMS, a footwear and accessories company known for its "One for One" business model. For every product purchased, TOMS donates a pair of shoes to a person in need. This socially conscious approach has resonated with consumers who prioritize giving back. By incorporating social impact into their business model, TOMS has gained customer loyalty and goodwill while making a significant difference in communities worldwide.

These case studies demonstrate that businesses can thrive by adopting ethical practices that prioritize customer satisfaction, social responsibility, and sustainability. By focusing on long-term goals and building positive relationships with customers and stakeholders, businesses can reap the rewards of a strong reputation, customer loyalty, and sustainable growth.

Lies and misleading information in business and sales not only have negative consequences for consumers but also harm the reputation and success of businesses. However, there are alternative strategies that businesses can adopt to achieve success and competitiveness without resorting to unethical practices. By providing quality products or services, delivering value and satisfaction, building customer loyalty and trust, and fostering innovation and excellence, businesses can cultivate positive relationships and long-term success. Through the examination of case studies, it is evident that ethical business practices can lead to sustainable growth and customer loyalty. By embracing these principles, businesses can contribute to a marketplace built on trust, transparency, and integrity.

Lies and misleading information have no place in the realm of business and sales. These unethical practices not only erode trust and respect but also come with significant long-term risks and costs for businesses. Throughout this discussion, we have delved into the ethical implications of such actions, examined the consequences they have on various stakeholders, and analysed real-life case studies that exemplify the detrimental effects of deceptive practices.

Ethics play a vital role in business conduct, shaping the relationships between businesses and their customers, as well as between businesses and their stakeholders. When lies and misleading information are used to manipulate consumers, it undermines the foundation of trust that is essential for healthy business transactions. Consumers rely on accurate and truthful information to make informed decisions about the products or services they purchase. When businesses deceive their customers, it not only leads to financial loss but can also have severe consequences on their health and well-being. For example, false claims about the safety or effectiveness of a product can put consumers' health at risk.

Moreover, the negative impact extends beyond consumers. Businesses engaged in deceptive practices suffer reputational damage, facing negative publicity and potential legal repercussions. A tarnished reputation not only leads to a loss of customer loyalty but can also result in financial losses and difficulties in attracting new customers.

Additionally, businesses that engage in deceptive practices may face legal consequences, such as lawsuits or regulatory penalties, further adding to the costs and risks associated with dishonesty.

By examining case studies, we have witnessed first-hand the harm caused to consumers, businesses, and society as a whole. Instances of false advertising, hidden fees, and manipulative marketing tactics have deceived and harmed unsuspecting customers. These case studies highlight the urgency for stricter regulations and ethical standards to combat these unethical practices. It is imperative for businesses to prioritize the well-being and welfare of their customers, ensuring that their actions are aligned with the principles of honesty, transparency, and fair treatment.

To create a fair and trustworthy marketplace, businesses must embrace alternative strategies for success that do not rely on lies and misleading information. One of the key strategies is to prioritize the delivery of quality products or services. By investing in research and development, businesses can ensure that their offerings meet or exceed customer expectations, building a reputation for reliability and customer satisfaction.

Delivering value and satisfaction is another crucial aspect. By adopting fair pricing practices, transparent communication, and customer-centric approaches, businesses can establish trust and confidence among their customers. When customers feel that they are getting genuine value for their money and are treated with respect, it strengthens the bond between businesses and consumers.

Building customer loyalty and trust should be a top priority for businesses. This can be achieved through open and honest communication, responsive customer service, and a commitment to resolving any issues promptly. By being transparent about their business practices, policies, and any changes that may affect customers, businesses can foster trust and loyalty that will contribute to long-term success.

Furthermore, fostering innovation and excellence can set businesses apart from their competitors. By embracing new technologies, investing in research and development, and staying ahead of industry trends, businesses can offer unique and valuable solutions to their customers. A focus on excellence in all aspects of operations, including customer service, manufacturing processes, and supply chain management, not only enhances the customer experience but also contributes to a positive brand image.

In conclusion, lies and misleading information have no place in business and sales. The consequences of such practices are far-reaching and detrimental, damaging trust, reputation, and customer relationships. To foster a fair and trustworthy marketplace, businesses must prioritize ethical conduct, transparency, and consumer welfare. By embracing alternative strategies that prioritize the delivery of quality products or services, delivering value and satisfaction, building customer loyalty and trust, and fostering innovation and excellence, businesses can build lasting relationships, maintain a positive reputation, and contribute to a more ethical and sustainable business environment.

Chapter 17

Detecting lies and misleading information is a complex task that investigative agencies tackle using various methods and methodologies. The effectiveness and reliability of these methods can vary depending on the specific circumstances and available resources. Let's explore some of the common techniques used and examine their strengths and limitations.

1. Polygraph tests: Polygraph tests, also known as lie detector tests, measure physiological responses such as heart rate, blood pressure,

respiration, and skin conductivity. The theory behind this method is that lying causes emotional arousal, leading to detectable changes in these physiological indicators. However, polygraph tests are not considered fool proof and have limitations. Factors like stress, anxiety, fear, or countermeasures can influence the results, potentially leading to false positives or false negatives. Consequently, their admissibility as evidence in courts and their acceptance within scientific communities are limited.

2. Voice stress analysis: Voice stress analysis involves examining vocal characteristics like pitch, frequency, amplitude, or micro tremors to detect signs of stress associated with lying. However, similar to polygraph tests, voice stress analysis is not widely accepted as a reliable method of detecting deception. It can be influenced by factors such as emotions, voice quality, speech rate, or background noise. Moreover, voice stress analysis is considered pseudoscience and lacks scientific evidence to support its validity.

3. Statement analysis: Statement analysis involves scrutinizing verbal or written statements for signs of deception, such as inconsistencies, contradictions, omissions, changes in tense or pronouns, qualifiers, or lack of details. The underlying assumption is that lying imposes a cognitive load on individuals, leading to observable linguistic features. While statement analysis can be a useful tool, it is subjective and prone to interpretation errors. Factors like memory, culture, personality, or communication style can affect the analysis, making it less reliable.

4. Behavioural analysis: Behavioural analysis focuses on observing nonverbal behaviour, including eye contact, facial expressions, gestures, posture, and movements, to detect potential cues of deception. This method relies on the belief that emotional leakage occurs when individuals lie, leading to discernible behavioural signs. However, similar to other methods, behavioural analysis has limitations. Baseline behaviour, context, motivation, and individual differences can all

impact the accuracy of interpreting behavioural cues. It requires skilled and trained professionals to accurately observe and analyse nonverbal behaviour.

It is important to note that no single method can guarantee 100% accuracy in detecting lies and deception. Investigative agencies typically employ a combination of methods and methodologies to gather and analyse information from different sources and perspectives. They rely on critical thinking and logical reasoning to evaluate the evidence and draw conclusions based on the preponderance of evidence.

In practice, investigators may employ additional techniques, such as forensic analysis of documents, financial audits, surveillance, witness interviews, or digital forensics, depending on the nature of the investigation. The integration of multiple approaches allows for a more comprehensive assessment of the veracity of information and helps mitigate the limitations of individual methods.

There are some drugs and medicines that have been used or experimented with for the purpose of making people reveal the truth and tell facts. These drugs and medicines are often called "truth drugs" or "truth serums", but they are not very reliable or effective in achieving their goal. Some of the drugs and medicines that have been used or experimented with as truth drugs are:

- Sodium thiopental: This is a barbiturate drug that was originally developed as an anesthetic, but was also found to make people more chatty and disinhibited when they were in a state of semi-consciousness. It was used by some police and military organizations in the 20th century to interrogate prisoners or suspects, but it was also found to be easily resisted or counteracted by some people, and to produce false or unreliable information from others.

The limitations and potential dangers of relying on drugs or medicines as truth serums can be seen through various case studies. One notable example is the use of sodium thiopental, commonly known as "truth serum." Despite its initial use in interrogations, studies have shown that its effects can vary widely among individuals. Some people may become more talkative and disinhibited, but others can resist its influence or provide false information under its influence.

- Scopolamine: This is a drug derived from a plant that has various effects on the nervous system, such as inducing drowsiness, amnesia, and suggestibility. It was used by some intelligence agencies in the 20th century to interrogate spies or enemies, but it was also found to be very dangerous and unpredictable, causing severe side effects such as hallucinations, psychosis, or death.

In the case of scopolamine, which was experimented with as a truth drug, the outcomes were even more concerning. While it can induce amnesia and suggestibility, it also poses severe risks to the individual's health and well-being. The unpredictable nature of its effects, including hallucinations and psychosis, makes it highly dangerous and unreliable for obtaining accurate information.

- Alcohol: This is a common drug that affects the brain and the body in various ways, such as impairing judgment, memory, and inhibition. It is often used by individuals to obtain information from others in a more innocent or casual way, but it is also used by some professionals to verify the reliability or loyalty of their agents or sources. However, alcohol is also known to distort or exaggerate information, and to affect different people differently.

Alcohol, although not specifically developed as a truth drug, is often used in social settings to loosen inhibitions and encourage people to share information more freely. However, it is well-known that alcohol impairs judgment, memory, and can lead to exaggeration or distortion of information. Thus, relying on alcohol to extract reliable facts can be highly misleading.

Cognitive interviewing is a valuable approach employed in forensic investigations to improve the accuracy of information obtained from witnesses or victims. By utilizing specific questioning techniques, cognitive interviewing aims to stimulate memory retrieval while minimizing the potential for misinformation. This method is considered an ethical and effective alternative for extracting the truth and facts from individuals.

The primary focus of cognitive interviewing is to establish a positive rapport and create a supportive environment that encourages open communication. By building trust and rapport with the interviewee, the technique aims to enhance their willingness to share accurate and detailed information. This approach recognizes the importance of respecting the individual's autonomy and ensuring their comfort throughout the interview process.

To maximize memory recall, cognitive interviewing employs various strategies. Open-ended questions are utilized to allow the interviewee to provide a comprehensive account of the event or situation under investigation. This technique encourages the interviewee to elaborate on their memories, providing additional context and details that may have been initially overlooked.

Furthermore, cognitive interviewing emphasizes the use of prompts and cues to aid memory retrieval. The interviewee is encouraged to mentally recreate the environment and emotions they experienced during the event, which can trigger a more vivid recollection of the relevant details. By focusing on sensory cues, such as sights, sounds, and smells, cognitive interviewing aims to facilitate accurate memory recall.

Importantly, cognitive interviewing also recognizes the potential for misinformation and takes steps to minimize its influence. Interviewers are trained to avoid suggestive questioning or leading statements that could inadvertently distort the interviewee's recollection. By maintaining neutrality and refraining from introducing preconceived notions, cognitive interviewing aims to preserve the integrity and accuracy of the information obtained.

Studies have demonstrated the effectiveness of cognitive interviewing in enhancing the retrieval of accurate information. Compared to traditional interview techniques, cognitive interviewing has been shown to improve the quality and quantity of information provided by witnesses and victims. Its emphasis on creating a supportive environment and utilizing memory retrieval strategies increases the likelihood of obtaining reliable and detailed accounts of events.

In contrast to the controversial use of drugs or invasive procedures, cognitive interviewing offers a morally and ethically sound approach to extracting information. By prioritizing the individual's well-being, autonomy, and the principles of informed consent, cognitive interviewing ensures a respectful and effective means of obtaining the truth and facts from individuals involved in forensic investigations.

In conclusion, cognitive interviewing stands as an essential technique for obtaining accurate information from witnesses and victims in forensic investigations. By employing specific questioning methods, building rapport, and minimizing the potential for misinformation, cognitive interviewing enhances memory recall while adhering to ethical principles. This approach offers a reliable and ethical alternative to the use of drugs or invasive procedures, promoting the integrity of the investigative process and the pursuit of truth.

Hypnosis: Hypnosis has been explored as a potential method to access repressed memories or uncover hidden information. However, its effectiveness and reliability in retrieving accurate information are highly debated, and its use is generally not considered reliable in legal or investigative contexts.

These are some of the drugs and medicines that have been used or experimented with as truth drugs, but none of them has proven to be very effective or reliable in making people reveal the truth and tell facts. In fact, most experts agree that there is no such thing as a perfect truth drug that can guarantee accurate information from an unwilling subject. The best way to obtain the truth from someone is still through careful questioning, observation, and verification.

In conclusion, detecting lies and misleading information is a complex process that requires the integration of multiple methods and approaches. While techniques like polygraph tests, voice stress analysis, statement analysis, and behavioural analysis are employed, they all have inherent limitations and should be used cautiously. Investigative agencies employ critical thinking, logical reasoning, and a range of investigative tools to gather evidence and make informed judgments. The key is to approach the task of detecting lies with a balanced perspective and an understanding of the strengths and limitations of each method.

Chapter 18

The presence of organized criminal networks and corrupt practices within the realms of healthcare and education, often referred to as the "medical and education mafia," is a grave concern that extends beyond geographical boundaries. These underground operations thrive through a web of lies and deception, exploiting vulnerabilities and preying upon unsuspecting individuals.

In the medical field, the mafia operates through various means, including fraudulent practices, illegal trafficking of medicines, counterfeit drugs, and even involvement in organ trafficking. They manipulate patients, medical professionals, and regulatory systems for personal gain. This can involve providing false diagnoses, prescribing unnecessary treatments or medications, and charging exorbitant fees. By capitalizing on people's desperation for quality healthcare, these criminal networks not only harm individuals physically and financially but also erode trust in the healthcare system as a whole.

Education is another sector that falls victim to the nefarious activities of the education mafia. These networks engage in a range of deceitful practices, such as running bogus educational institutions, selling fake degrees or diplomas, and orchestrating admission scams. They exploit the aspirations of students and their families, offering false promises of quality education and lucrative career opportunities. This not only leads to financial losses for individuals but also devalues the integrity of educational qualifications and undermines the credibility of legitimate educational institutions.

The tactics employed by the medical and education mafia are often sophisticated and well-coordinated. They involve creating complex networks of individuals who collaborate to carry out their illicit activities while evading detection and legal repercussions. These networks may involve professionals within the respective industries, corrupt officials, and even organized crime syndicates.

The impact of the medical and education mafia is far-reaching. It perpetuates inequality, as those with greater financial means can bypass regulations and gain access to better healthcare or educational opportunities. It also undermines social and economic development, as resources meant for the improvement of these sectors are siphoned off through fraudulent practices. Additionally, the erosion of trust in medical and educational institutions hampers progress in public health, scientific research, and educational advancement.

Addressing the challenges posed by the medical and education mafia requires a multi-faceted approach. It involves strengthening regulatory frameworks, enhancing oversight mechanisms, and promoting transparency and accountability. Collaboration between law enforcement agencies, regulatory bodies, and international organizations is crucial to combating these criminal networks. Additionally, raising awareness among the general public about the risks and warning signs associated with these illegal practices is essential to empower individuals to make informed decisions.

Efforts to combat the medical and education mafia must prioritize the protection of vulnerable individuals, including patients, students, and their families. Providing support systems and avenues for reporting fraud and corruption can help victims seek justice and deter future criminal activities. Moreover, fostering a culture of integrity and ethical practices within the medical and education sectors is vital to rebuild trust and ensure the delivery of quality services.

While the medical and education mafia continues to pose significant challenges worldwide, concerted efforts to expose and dismantle these networks can help create a safer and more equitable environment for both healthcare and education.

Chapter 19

During times of war, lies and deceptions often find their place, stemming from the inherent complexities of conflict, violence, and the difficult task of justifying or explaining such circumstances. The reasons behind the prevalence of lies and deceptions during war are diverse and intriguing:

- Mobilizing public support becomes a crucial motive for war leaders who resort to lies or deception regarding the causes, goals, or progress of the war. Their aim is to gain or sustain public approval, boost morale, and foster patriotism. An example of this can be seen in the 2003 invasion of Iraq by the United States and its allies, where false claims of Iraq possessing weapons of mass destruction and links to al Qaeda were used as justifications.[1]

- Deceiving the enemy becomes a strategic tactic employed by war fighters to gain an advantage, achieve surprise, or secure victory. Lies and deceptions are utilized to mislead the enemy about intentions, capabilities, or strategies. A classic illustration of this is Operation Fortitude, initiated by the Allies in 1944, which utilized deception to misguide the Germans regarding the timing and location of the D-Day invasion.

- Concealing atrocities represents a dark aspect of lies and deceptions during war. Perpetrators engage in falsehoods to hide their involvement in or responsibility for atrocities such as massacres, torture, or genocide. Their aim is to evade accountability, condemnation, or intervention. A chilling example occurred in 1995 when Bosnian Serb forces killed over 8,000 Bosnian Muslim men and boys in Srebrenica. They vehemently denied their role and attempted to cover up the evidence.

- Coping with trauma becomes an intimate motive for war survivors who resort to lies or deceptions regarding their experiences, feelings, or actions during the war. This internal deception serves as a mechanism to cope with the trauma, guilt, or shame inflicted upon them. For instance, certain Vietnam veterans may have fabricated tales of heroism or suffering to grapple with the profound psychological wounds they endured.

While these examples shed light on the prevalence of lies and deceptions during war, it is important to note that not everyone involved in war engages in continuous or extensive deception. Context, individual motivations, and variations in the frequency and severity of deception play significant roles. Furthermore, lying and deceiving during war carry ethical and legal implications and consequences that should not be overlooked.

Intriguingly, the realm of war exposes a complex web of truths and untruths, where narratives are skilfully crafted to navigate the turbulent waters of conflict. Understanding the multifaceted nature of lies and deceptions during war allows us to critically analyse the ethical dilemmas they present, explore avenues for accountability, and work towards a world where truth can prevail even amidst the chaos of war.

Chapter 20

The ethical acceptance and moral rightness of lies and deception is a contentious and debated topic. In general, honesty and truthfulness are considered fundamental ethical principles that should guide human behaviour. However, there are some situations where lying or deception may be argued to be ethically acceptable or morally right, depending on the circumstances and the ethical framework being applied. Here are a few scenarios that are often discussed in this context:

1. Protection of life: In certain situations, lying or deceiving someone may be seen as justifiable if it is done to protect someone's life. For example, lying to an oppressor about the whereabouts of a person who is being hunted down for their political beliefs could be considered morally right if it prevents harm or death.

2. Maintaining confidentiality: Professionals, such as therapists, doctors, or lawyers, are often bound by confidentiality agreements or

legal obligations to keep information confidential. In some cases, this may require withholding or misleading information from others, but it is seen as ethically acceptable to protect the privacy and well-being of individuals.

3. Preserving surprises or gifts: Lying or deception can be seen as morally acceptable in situations where it is intended to preserve a surprise or enhance someone's enjoyment. For example, hiding the details of a surprise birthday party or keeping a secret gift can be considered harmless and even a thoughtful gesture.

4. Preserving cultural or social norms: In certain cultures or societies, there may be situations where lying or deception is considered morally right to maintain harmony, avoid conflicts, or uphold cultural norms. For instance, in some cultures, it is common to use polite lies or deception to spare someone's feelings or maintain social cohesion.

It is important to note that these examples are not universally accepted as morally right in all ethical frameworks, and opinions can vary. Ethical considerations often involve a balance between competing values and principles, and the specific circumstances and potential consequences should be carefully evaluated. Ultimately, the assessment of when lying or deception may be considered ethically acceptable or morally right depends on individual perspectives and the ethical framework being applied.

Chapter 21

Once upon a time, in the enchanting town of Indianaville, a dark cloud of corruption and deceit loomed over its unsuspecting residents. In the heart of this picturesque town, a renowned politician named Robert Indiana had fallen from grace. He stood accused of accepting bribes and shamelessly lying under oath, betraying the very trust placed in him by the people.

The air was heavy with tension as the courtroom doors creaked open, revealing the scene that would forever change the destiny of Indianaville. Inside, a palpable sense of anticipation gripped the onlookers, their eyes fixated on the towering figure of justice, Lady Justice herself, who presided over the proceedings.

It was in this crucible of truth and falsehood that two unlikely heroes emerged, James and Emily. James, a brilliant psychologist, possessed an unyielding determination to uncover the deepest truths hidden within the human psyche. Emily, a passionate and tenacious lawyer, fought fiercely for justice, wielding her words as weapons against the web of lies that threatened to ensnare their beloved town.

As the trial unfolded, James became acutely aware of the insidious nature of deception and the dire consequences it had on the lives of innocent individuals. His soul burned with an unquenchable fire; ignited by the injustice he witnessed first-hand. He knew that the frail foundation upon which lie detection stood had to be shattered, replaced by a new paradigm that would pierce through the darkest recesses of deceit.

Emily, with her unwavering gaze and unwavering resolve, understood the weight of her duty. She saw the anguish etched on the faces of the townspeople, their trust shattered by the actions of their once-revered leader. Determined to restore their faith, she joined forces with James, believing that their combined expertise held the key to unravelling the tangled web of lies that threatened to suffocate Indianaville.

Together, they embarked on a perilous journey, their quest for truth taking them into uncharted territories of the human psyche. They traversed treacherous landscapes of doubt and scepticism, their every step a testament to their unwavering conviction. The weight of the town's hopes and dreams rested upon their shoulders, and failure was not an option.

Countless sleepless nights and tireless days were spent poring over mountains of data, as James and Emily sought to unravel the mysteries of lie detection. Their research became a battleground of scientific inquiry, as they grappled with the demons of doubt and the spectre of failure. But they pressed on, their passion fuelling their every endeavour.

News of their ground-breaking work spread like wildfire, igniting a flicker of hope within the hearts of the townspeople. Their excitement grew as whispers of a new dawn of justice echoed through the streets of Indianaville. James and Emily became beacons of hope, symbols of resilience in the face of adversity.

Finally, the day arrived when they would present their findings to the court. The air crackled with electricity, anticipation clinging to every breath. As James and Emily took their place on the witness stand, their eyes burned with a fierce determination, their voices ringing with unwavering conviction.

In a crescendo of emotion and dramatization, they delivered their testimony, each word a battle cry against the tyranny of deception. Their voices carried the weight of their research, their hearts poured into every syllable, their expertise resonating with the raw power of truth.

The courtroom stood still, their eyes locked on James and Emily, hanging on to their every word. The jury and the judge, captivated by the magnitude of their research, saw a glimmer of hope amidst the darkness that had shrouded their beloved town.

As James and Emily concluded their testimony, a profound silence descended upon the courtroom. The weight of their words reverberated through the hearts and minds of every individual present. And in that moment, they knew they had unleashed a tidal wave of change, forever altering the course of justice in Indianaville.

The jury, enlightened by their research, deliberated with newfound clarity. The truth, like a beacon amidst the storm, guided their every thought. The verdict was reached—a resounding declaration of guilt for Robert Indiana. The town exhaled a collective breath, releasing the burdens of doubt and uncertainty that had plagued them for far too long.

In the aftermath of their triumph, James and Emily stood as pillars of justice in Indianaville. The townspeople, forever grateful for their unwavering dedication, bestowed upon them a legacy that would be etched into the annals of their town's history.

James and Emily's story became the stuff of legends, whispered with reverence and awe in the hallowed halls of justice. Their journey embodied the triumph of perseverance and the indomitable spirit of those who dared to challenge the status quo.

And in the hearts of the people of Indianaville, James and Emily would forever remain as symbols of hope, their names eternally intertwined with the renaissance of truth and the triumph of justice.

Research on lie detection, particularly in the context of psychology and law, has been extensively studied over the past few decades. This interest stems from the prevalence of lying in our daily lives, both personally and professionally, as well as the historical use of lies by public figures. However, the primary motivation for studying lie detection scientifically has been the detrimental impact of lying in court, which threatens fair trials and the rule of law. False testimonies can lead to the conviction of innocent individuals or the exoneration of guilty ones, and there have been documented cases of innocent people being wrongly convicted due to lying witnesses.

When evaluating the truthfulness of a testimony, the court considers various factors such as other evidence, known facts about the case, and testimonies from other witnesses. Inconsistencies with physical evidence or other witness accounts can indicate dishonesty, but they can also result from normal human errors in observation and memory. In situations where the facts of the case are not well known, witness testimonies, especially from those with a personal stake, can play a critical role in reaching a verdict. While perjury charges exist for witnesses lying in court, there are still instances where witnesses provide false testimony. In such cases, determining the credibility of witnesses becomes crucial for the court's decision. This raises the question of whether it is possible to identify liars and truth-tellers based on their non-verbal behaviour.

Common beliefs about lying and deceit include the association of certain non-verbal cues with dishonesty, such as gaze avoidance, fidgeting, and changes in body posture. These beliefs are not only held by the general public but also by professionals in law and psychology. Many countries offer courses and programs that claim to teach lie detection skills, such as identifying deception through behaviour analysis in airport security (SPOT program) or in legal settings (SYNEROLOGY program). However, empirical research spanning several decades has consistently shown that none of the assumed non-verbal cues reliably indicate lying or truthfulness. The widely popularized notion of facial micro-expressions as indicators of lies, promoted by courses and training programs, lacks scientific support.

Studies have consistently demonstrated that people's ability to detect lies based on non-verbal cues is mediocre at best. Meta-analyses of veracity judgments have shown that the average accuracy is at chance level, with professionals such as police investigators and psychiatrists performing no better than laypersons. Field studies, including interviews with suspects and interviews with mourning relatives of victims, have also yielded poor results in distinguishing truthfulness. Deception detection programs based on behaviour analysis, aimed at identifying individuals with malicious intentions, have failed scientific tests.

The research field focused on uncovering non-verbal cues to deception faces several challenges. The literature suffers from structural issues, including flexibility in coding cues, selective reporting of significant findings, and an overrepresentation of significant results. Even if some cues weakly indicate deception, the current body of research may be biased and unreliable. While non-verbal cues may shed light on other aspects of human communication and interaction, their application in forensic lie detection is unlikely to be fruitful.

The research field now faces the question of its future direction. Should it continue searching for reliable non-verbal cues or focus on combinations of cues? Some suggest defining terms more precisely or improving the measurement of non-verbal cues, while others recommend increasing study power through larger sample sizes. However, these strategies may be impractical in forensic contexts. Small effects, even if statistically significant, may not provide reliable individual-level or statement-level lie detection. Moreover, the theoretical foundations of non-verbal cues to deception are shaky, and the possibility that the basic premise of the inquiry is false has not been fully acknowledged.

Individual differences in lie detection judgments are influenced by various factors, including genetics, culture, personal experiences, and situational factors.

Chapter 22

Once upon a time in a quaint little town lived three friends named Nalini, Shyam, and Radhika. They were known for their close bond and shared a passion for storytelling. Each had their unique storytelling style, captivating their audience with their imaginative tales.

Nalini was a vivacious and charismatic storyteller. With a twinkle in her eyes, she weaved enchanting stories that transported her listeners to magical realms. She possessed a remarkable ability to make her narratives feel real, and her audience couldn't help but get lost in the world she created.

Shyam, on the other hand, had a more analytical approach to storytelling. He preferred to unravel complex plots and explore the depths of human emotions. His tales were thought-provoking, often leaving the audience reflecting on their own lives and choices. His words had a way of piercing through the hearts of his listeners, touching them on a profound level.

Radhika, the third member of their storytelling trio, had a penchant for suspense and mystery. Her stories were filled with twists and turns, keeping her audience on the edge of their seats. She had a gift for crafting intricate narratives that left her listeners guessing until the very end. Radhika's tales were like puzzles waiting to be solved, and her audience eagerly awaited each new revelation.

As the years went by, their storytelling prowess grew, and they became popular figures in their town. People would gather around, eagerly anticipating the moment when Nalini, Shyam, or Radhika would start spinning their tales. Their friendship was strengthened by their shared passion, and they constantly challenged each other to push the boundaries of their storytelling abilities.

However, beneath the surface of their harmonious friendship, self-deception began to weave its web. Nalini, enthralled by the admiration she received for her stories, started to believe she was a better storyteller than her friends. She began to subtly undermine Shyam and Radhika, casting doubt on their abilities whenever she had the chance.

Meanwhile, Shyam, aware of Nalini's growing ego, sought solace in his own self-deception. He convinced himself that his stories were far superior to Nalini's and that he was the true master of their storytelling trio. In his mind, he believed that Radhika's stories lacked depth and complexity, overshadowing her contributions.

Radhika, too, fell victim to self-deception. She convinced herself that her suspenseful tales were the epitome of storytelling brilliance. She dismissed Nalini's enchanting narratives as mere tricks to captivate the audience, failing to acknowledge the genuine magic they contained. In her eyes, Shyam's introspective tales lacked the thrill she believed to be essential.

Unbeknownst to each other, their self-deceptions festered, poisoning the once pure and supportive friendship they shared. Their once collaborative storytelling sessions turned into fierce competitions, each trying to outshine the other. Their words, once crafted to inspire and entertain, now carried an air of arrogance and superiority.

One day, as the town eagerly awaited their storytelling performance, Nalini, Shyam, and Radhika found themselves unable to create their usual magic. The essence of their stories seemed lost, and the once captivated audience was left disappointed. It was as if their self-deception had drained the very life out of their creativity.

Realizing the impact of their self-deceptions, they confronted each other, acknowledging their flaws and the damage they had caused. In that moment of honesty, they rediscovered the essence of their friendship and the power of collaboration. They understood that self-deception had clouded their judgment and hindered their growth as storytellers.

With renewed humility and a desire to reconnect with their true passion, they set out to create a story together. Combining Nalini's enchantment, Shyam's depth, and Radhika's suspense, they crafted a tale that captured the hearts and minds of their audience once again. It was a story that celebrated their individual talents while highlighting the beauty of their collective efforts.

From that day forward, Nalini, Shyam, and Radhika continued their storytelling journey together, embracing the diversity of their styles and valuing each other's contributions. They learned that true greatness lies not in self-deception but in the ability to recognize and appreciate the unique gifts of others.

And so, their stories lived on, touching the souls of those who listened, reminding them of the power of unity, humility, and the magic that can be created when hearts and minds intertwine in harmony.

Self-deception is a common phenomenon that can lead us to believe our own lies and make us more convincing to others. It is observed in various contexts, including fraud and unethical behaviour, where individuals deceive themselves to protect their self-image and maintain a clear conscience. Self-deception can also help us justify potential conflicts of interest in our work and enhance our persuasive abilities.

Studies have shown that self-deception can boost our egos and make us believe we are smarter or more capable than we actually are. For example, participants in experiments showed inflated confidence in their abilities, even when they knew they had relied on cheating or fraudulent data. Self-deception can also influence our personal beliefs and opinions, especially when we need to argue a point or persuade others.

Researchers have found that self-deception is unconscious and happens below conscious awareness, making it challenging to study scientifically. However, experiments have revealed that self-deception can have significant effects on decision-making and behaviour. By understanding the factors contributing to self-deception, we can become more aware of its influence on our own decisions and prevent it from leading us astray.

Self-deception can be driven by a desire to protect our self-image, justify our actions, and increase our persuasiveness. It can lead to delusions of grandeur, where we believe we are smarter, more moral, or more convincing than we actually are. Recognizing and addressing our own self-deception can help us make more informed and ethical choices in various aspects of life, including work and relationships.

Chapter 23

Lying to oneself is a profound act of self-deception, wherein one deliberately convinces them of something that is untrue or only partially true. Engaging in self-deception can have detrimental effects, as it hinders one's ability to confront reality, learn from past mistakes, and undergo personal growth. Recognizing whether we are deceiving ourselves requires careful introspection and self-awareness. Here are some indicators that can help us identify instances of self-deception:

First and foremost, paying attention to our emotions can provide valuable insights. If we experience discomfort, anxiety, guilt, or defensiveness when contemplating or discussing a specific subject, it may indicate that we are not being honest with ourselves about it. Additionally, cognitive dissonance, that uneasy mental state resulting from a conflict between our beliefs or actions, may manifest itself.

Our thoughts can also serve as a revealing mirror of self-deception. Rationalizing, justifying, minimizing, or avoiding certain thoughts or facts may be a signal that we are deceiving ourselves. We might notice that our thoughts are vague, inconsistent, or even contradictory, reflecting our attempt to maintain the illusion we have constructed.

Examining our behaviour can offer further insights into self-deception. If our actions do not align with our deeply held values, goals, or aspirations, it may suggest that we are deceiving ourselves about our true desires and needs. Engaging in self-sabotaging behaviours, such as procrastination, avoidance, or escapism, can be indicative of this internal deception.

Feedback from others can also serve as a potent tool for self-reflection. When we receive feedback that challenges or contradicts our self-image, beliefs, or opinions, it may point to areas where we are deceiving ourselves. It is not uncommon to instinctively ignore, dismiss, or reject such feedback rather than genuinely considering it or learning from it.

It is crucial to recognize that these signs of self-deception are not absolute and may vary depending on the individual and the circumstances at hand. Therefore, cultivating an open-minded and inquisitive attitude towards ourselves and our reality becomes paramount. We must be willing to engage in honest self-examination and seek support and guidance when needed. Embracing the truth about ourselves is not a sign of weakness; rather, it demonstrates strength and authenticity, enabling us to live more purposefully and meaningfully.

From a philosophical perspective, self-deception raises profound questions about the nature of truth, the human capacity for self-awareness, and the limits of our understanding. It confronts us with the complexities of human consciousness and the intricate ways in which our minds construct and interpret reality. Engaging in self-deception can be seen as a defence mechanism, an attempt to shield ourselves from uncomfortable truths or preserve a desired self-image. However, by doing so, we inevitably distort our perception of reality and hinder our personal growth.

Socrates, the renowned philosopher of ancient Greece, emphasized the importance of self-examination and the pursuit of self-knowledge. He famously declared, "Know thyself." This maxim underscores the fundamental significance of truth-seeking and self-awareness in leading a virtuous and fulfilling life. By deceiving ourselves, we deviate from Socratic wisdom, inhibiting our ability to understand ourselves and the world around us.

Existential philosophers such as Jean-Paul Sartre and Friedrich Nietzsche explored the concept of authenticity, which is intimately tied to facing the truth about oneself. Sartre posited that authenticity requires individuals to acknowledge the responsibility they hold for their choices and to confront the inherent uncertainties and anxieties of existence. In contrast, Nietzsche warned against the dangers of self-deception, urging individuals to embrace the harsh realities of life and assert their will to power.

From a pragmatic standpoint, confronting our self-deception is crucial for personal growth and development. Only by acknowledging and accepting the truth about ourselves can we embark on a genuine journey of self-improvement and fulfilment. It is through this process that we confront our weaknesses, learn from our mistakes, and strive towards a more authentic and meaningful existence.

In conclusion, self-deception is a complex and profound phenomenon that can hinder our personal growth and authenticity. Recognizing the signs of self-deception requires introspection, attentiveness to our emotions, thoughts, behaviours, and feedback from others. Approaching this endeavour with an open mind and a commitment to truth-seeking enables us to live more honestly and meaningfully. Philosophically, self-deception raises questions about the nature of truth, the human capacity for self-awareness, and the pursuit of authenticity. By embracing self-examination and facing the truth about ourselves, we embark on a path of personal growth, fostering a deeper understanding of our existence and enabling us to live in alignment with our true selves.

Chapter 24

The ethical acceptance and moral rightness of lies and deception is a contentious and debated topic. In general, honesty and truthfulness are considered fundamental ethical principles that should guide human behaviour. However, there are some situations where lying or deception may be argued to be ethically acceptable or morally right, depending on the circumstances and the ethical framework being applied. In this text, we will first define what lying and deception are, and how they differ from each other. Then, we will explain what ethical frameworks are, and how they can be used to evaluate the morality of lying and deception. Finally, we will present some of the main arguments for and against lying and deception from different ethical perspectives.

1. Definition of lying and deception: Lying is usually defined as making a statement that one believes to be false with the intention of deceiving someone. Deception is a wider concept that includes any act or omission that causes someone to believe something that one believes to be false. Deception can be done by words, actions, or inactions. For example, lying is a form of verbal deception, while hiding something or wearing a disguise are forms of non-verbal deception.

2. Ethical frameworks for lying and deception: Ethical frameworks are systems of principles, values, or rules that guide moral reasoning and decision-making. Some of the common ethical frameworks are deontology, consequentialism, virtue ethics, and care ethics. Each framework has its own criteria for determining the rightness or wrongness of an action, such as the duty, the consequence, the character, or the relationship involved. Ethical frameworks can help us analyse the morality of lying and deception by applying their criteria to specific cases or scenarios.

3. Arguments for and against lying and deception: Here are some examples of scenarios where lying or deception may be argued to be ethically acceptable or morally right, and some of the arguments for and against them from different ethical perspectives:

- Protection of life: In certain situations, lying or deceiving someone may be seen as justifiable if it is done to protect someone's life. For example, lying to an oppressor about the whereabouts of a person who is being hunted down for their political beliefs could be considered morally right if it prevents harm or death.

- Deontology: This framework argues that lying is always wrong because it violates the duty of respect for rational beings and their autonomy. Lying treats people as means rather than ends in them, and undermines their ability to make free and informed choices. Therefore, lying is not ethically acceptable even if it protects someone's life.

- Consequentialism: This framework argues that lying can be right or wrong depending on its consequences for the overall happiness or well-being of those affected. Lying is ethically acceptable if it produces better than harm, and morally wrong if it produces more harm than good. Therefore, lying can be ethically acceptable if it protects someone's life.

- Virtue ethics: This framework argues that lying is wrong because it corrupts the character of the liar and undermines the trustworthiness of human relationships. Lying goes against the virtues of honesty, integrity, and fidelity, which are essential for moral excellence and flourishing. Therefore, lying is not ethically acceptable even if it protects someone's life.

- Care ethics: This framework argues that lying can be right or wrong depending on the context and the nature of the relationship between the liar and the deceived. Lying is ethically acceptable if it expresses care, compassion, or empathy for someone who is vulnerable or in need, and morally wrong if it expresses indifference, hostility, or exploitation. Therefore, lying can be ethically acceptable if it protects someone's life.

- Maintaining confidentiality: Professionals, such as therapists, doctors, or lawyers, are often bound by confidentiality agreements or legal obligations to keep information confidential. In some cases, this may require withholding or misleading information from others, but it is seen as ethically acceptable to protect the privacy and well-being of individuals.

- Deontology: This framework argues that withholding or misleading information is not necessarily lying, as long as it does not involve making a false statement with the intention of deceiving someone. Withholding or misleading information can be seen as respecting the autonomy and dignity of individuals who have entrusted their information to professionals.

Therefore, withholding or misleading information is ethically acceptable to maintain confidentiality.

- Consequentialism: This framework argues that withholding or misleading information can be right or wrong depending on its consequences for the overall happiness or well-being of those affected. Withholding or misleading information is ethically acceptable if it prevents harm or promotes good for the individuals who have shared their information with professionals, and morally wrong if it causes harm or reduces good for them or others.

Therefore, withholding or misleading information is ethically acceptable to maintain confidentiality.

- Virtue ethics: This framework argues that withholding or misleading information is wrong because it violates the virtues of honesty, integrity, and fidelity, which are essential for moral excellence and flourishing. Withholding or misleading information goes against the moral obligation to be truthful and loyal to others, and erodes the trust and respect that are the basis of human relationships.

Therefore, withholding or misleading information is not ethically acceptable to maintain confidentiality.

- Care ethics: This framework argues that withholding or misleading information can be right or wrong depending on the context and the nature of the relationship between the professionals and the individuals who have shared their information with them.

Withholding or misleading information is ethically acceptable if it expresses care, compassion, or empathy for the individuals who are vulnerable or in need, and morally wrong if it expresses indifference, hostility, or exploitation.

Therefore, withholding or misleading information is ethically acceptable to maintain confidentiality.

- Preserving surprises or gifts: Lying or deception can be seen as morally acceptable in situations where it is intended to preserve a surprise or enhance someone's enjoyment. For example, hiding the details of a surprise birthday party or keeping a secret gift can be considered harmless and even a thoughtful gesture.

- Deontology: This framework argues that lying is always wrong because it violates the duty of respect for rational beings and their autonomy. Lying treats people as means rather than ends in them, and undermines their ability to make free and informed choices. Therefore, lying is not ethically acceptable even if it preserves surprises or gifts.

- Consequentialism: This framework argues that lying can be right or wrong depending on its consequences for the overall happiness or well-being of those affected. Lying is ethically acceptable if it produces better than harm, and morally wrong if it produces more harm than good. Therefore, lying can be ethically acceptable if it preserves surprises or gifts.

- Virtue ethics: This framework argues that lying is wrong because it corrupts the character of the liar and undermines the trustworthiness of human relationships. Lying goes against the virtues of honesty, integrity, and fidelity, which are essential for moral excellence and flourishing. However, this framework also recognizes that there may be exceptions to this rule, such as when lying is done out of kindness, generosity, or benevolence. Therefore, lying may be ethically acceptable if it preserves surprises or gifts.

- Care ethics: This framework argues that lying can be right or wrong depending on the context and the nature of the relationship between the liar and the deceived. Lying is ethically acceptable if it expresses care, compassion, or empathy for someone who is vulnerable or in need, and morally wrong if it expresses indifference, hostility, or exploitation. Therefore, lying can be ethically acceptable if it preserves surprises or gifts.

- Preserving cultural or social norms: In certain cultures or societies, there may be situations where lying or deception is considered morally right to maintain harmony, avoid conflicts, or uphold cultural norms. For example, in some cultures, it is common to use polite lies or deception to spare someone's feelings or maintain social cohesion.

- Deontology: This framework argues that lying is always wrong because it violates the duty of respect for rational beings and their autonomy. Lying treats people as means rather than ends in them, and undermines their ability to make free and informed choices. Therefore, lying is not ethically acceptable even if it preserves cultural or social norms.

- Consequentialism: This framework argues that lying can be right or wrong depending on its consequences for the overall happiness or well-being of those affected. Lying is ethically acceptable if it produces better than harm, and morally wrong if it produces more harm than good. Therefore, lying can be ethically acceptable if it preserves cultural or social norms.

- Virtue ethics: This framework argues that lying is wrong because it corrupts the character of the liar and undermines the trustworthiness of human relationships. Lying goes against the virtues of honesty, integrity, and fidelity, which are essential for moral excellence and flourishing. However, this framework also recognizes that there may be exceptions to this rule, such as when lying is done out of respect, courtesy, or prudence. Therefore, lying may be ethically acceptable if it preserves cultural or social norms.

- Care ethics: This framework argues that lying can be right or wrong depending on the context and the nature of the relationship between the liar and the deceived. Lying is ethically acceptable if it expresses care, compassion, or empathy for someone who is vulnerable or in need, and morally wrong if it expresses indifference, hostility, or exploitation. Therefore, lying can be ethically acceptable if it preserves cultural or social norms.

Finally, it should be noted that the moral justification for lying and deceit is a hotly contested issue. In general, it is believed that the fundamental ethical standards that should direct human behaviour are honesty and truthfulness. Nevertheless, depending on the circumstances and the ethical framework being used, there are some instances where lying or deception may be justified as morally correct or ethically acceptable. We've discussed what lying and deceit are as well as the differences between the two. We have defined ethical frameworks and discussed how they might be applied to assess the morality of lying and deceit. We have discussed some of the most important justifications for and against lying and deceit from many ethical viewpoints.

Chapter 25

In the bustling city of Mumbai, there existed a neighbourhood where Mr. Arjun and Mr. Asathya were next-door neighbors. Mr. Arjun, renowned for his sharp wit and astute observations, had a knack for unravelling the truth. On the other hand, Mr. Asathya, a notorious trickster, possessed a silver tongue and a fondness for deception.

One bright morning, as Mr. Arjun tended to his balcony garden, he caught sight of Mr. Asathya striding by with an air of self-importance. Unable to resist a bit of playful banter, Mr. Arjun called out to his neighbour.

"Ah, Mr. Asathya, my dear friend! What a pleasant surprise to see you today. Pray, enlighten me, have you recently spotted any Bollywood stars dancing in your backyard?"

Mr. Asathya chuckled, thoroughly entertained by Mr. Arjun's humorous sarcasm. "Oh, Mr. Arjun, you have such an imaginative mind. Bollywood stars in my backyard? That's quite a stretch!"

With a mischievous gleam in his eyes, Mr. Arjun continued, "Ah, my dear Asathya, it seems your storytelling skills are truly exceptional. But do you recall our conversation just yesterday when you claimed to have befriended Shah Rukh Khan at a local café?"

Mr. Asathya's face turned slightly crimson, his eyes darting nervously. "Ah, well, you see, Arjun, that was merely a jest. A playful exaggeration, if you will. You know how I love spinning tales!"

Raising an eyebrow, Mr. Arjun feigned surprise. "Oh, a jest, you say? Well, I must applaud your creative prowess. But I must admit, I was rather looking forward to a star-studded coffee date."

Mr. Asathya let out a nervous laugh, attempting to change the subject. "Oh, Arjun, you always take things too seriously! Let's not dwell on such trivial matters. Tell me, have you heard the gossip about aliens landing in Juhu Beach?"

Mr. Arjun burst into laughter, fully aware of Mr. Asathya's attempt to divert the conversation. "Ah, the aliens! How intriguing! But forgive me, my dear friend, I find my attention captivated by a different extraordinary sight. You see, just yesterday, I spotted a talking monkey swinging from your balcony."

Mr. Asathya's face paled, his web of deceit unravelling before him. "A talking monkey? Surely you must be mistaken, Arjun!"

Mr. Arjun chuckled mischievously. "Oh, dear Asathya, I have a keen eye for detail. This monkey, you see, had a striking resemblance to your mannerisms and seemed to possess an uncanny knowledge of your little fabrications."

Caught in his own web of lies, Mr. Asathya stammered, "Well, Arjun, I suppose it's time for me to come clean. Yes, I may have embellished a few stories here and there, but it was all in good fun, you know."

Mr. Arjun's laughter echoed through the Mumbai neighbourhood as he playfully patted Mr. Asathya on the back. "Oh, my dear friend, you never fail to entertain. But remember, the truth has a way of catching up with us. Perhaps it's time for a new chapter in the book of Asathya, one filled with honesty and authenticity."

From that day forward, Mr. Asathya learned the value of truthfulness, and Mumbai became an even livelier city with his comical tales of real-life adventures.

And Mr. Arjun continued to be the guardian of honesty, always ready to expose any more whimsical fibs that might come his neighbour's way, all in the spirit of good-natured laughter and friendship.

Chapter 26

People engage in the art of fabricating lies and meticulously constructing evidence to support their falsehoods for a myriad of reasons. The motives behind these deceptive acts are as diverse as the individuals themselves:

One common incentive for lying is the desire for personal gain. Some individuals deceive others in pursuit of financial rewards, power dynamics, or elevated social status. The allure of these benefits drives them to weave intricate webs of deceit.

Another motivation for fabricating lies is the avoidance of negative consequences. Whether it is evading punishment, deflecting blame, or sidestepping potential embarrassment, individuals resort to falsehoods as a means of self-preservation.

In some cases, lying serves as a shield to protect or enhance one's self-image. People may engage in deceit to boost their ego, conceal their insecurities, or construct rationalizations that justify their actions. By crafting an alternate version of reality, they create a facade that aligns with their desired self-perception.

Lying can also serve as a coping mechanism in the face of challenging situations. The act of deceiving others can alleviate stress, anxiety, or guilt, providing temporary relief from the emotional burdens that accompany difficult circumstances.

Furthermore, some individuals employ lies as tools of influence and manipulation. By fabricating false narratives, they seek to sway the opinions, emotions, or behaviours of others. Through carefully constructed falsehoods, they aim to shape the world around them to their advantage.

Those who engage in the act of fabricating lies and creating evidence employ various strategies to lend credibility to their falsehoods. These tactics are designed to make their lies appear more plausible and convincing:

One such strategy is repetition. By repeating the lie consistently, individuals create an illusion of truth. This technique capitalizes on the human tendency to associate repetition with validity, gradually eroding scepticism and embedding the lie into the collective consciousness.

Selective presentation of evidence is another commonly employed tactic. Liars often cherry-pick information, seeking out or presenting only supportive evidence while conveniently ignoring or dismissing anything that contradicts their falsehoods. This manipulation of the available data serves to bolster their narrative and make it appear more substantiated.

Distortion and exaggeration of facts also play a role in the construction of convincing lies. By bending the truth and stretching its boundaries, liars shape the narrative to align with their desired outcome. This manipulation of facts can make their deceit more compelling, as it appeals to confirmation biases and preconceived notions.

The omission or denial of relevant information is another tool in the liar's arsenal. By deliberately excluding or denying facts that contradict their falsehoods, individuals create a skewed perspective that aligns with their fabricated narrative. This deliberate act of deception aims to further solidify their false claims.

To enhance the persuasiveness of their lies, individuals often appeal to emotions, authority, or social norms. They exploit these psychological triggers to manipulate the perceptions and beliefs of others. By tugging at heartstrings, invoking the influence of authoritative figures, or leveraging societal expectations, liars strive to elicit compliance and belief.

Credibility plays a vital role in the success of a lie. Liars employ confident and consistent verbal and nonverbal cues to bolster their perceived credibility. Through the use of unwavering eye contact, assured body language, and a convincing tone, they seek to create an impression of trustworthiness and reliability.

However, the act of fabricating lies and creating evidence is not without its perils. The repercussions can be far-reaching and impact both the liar and those entangled in their deceit:

One notable consequence is the erosion of trust and relationships. Lies undermine the foundation of trust upon which healthy human connections thrive. Once trust is shattered, it becomes a daunting task to rebuild the bonds that have been severed.

Lying can also impair judgment and decision-making processes. The distorted Perception of reality that arises from deceit can cloud one's ability to make sound choices. The reliance on fabricated evidence can lead to misguided conclusions and flawed reasoning.

Furthermore, lies have the potential to distort both personal perception and collective memory. The malleability of memory combined with the influence of falsehoods can lead individuals to internalize and perpetuate inaccurate information, perpetuating a cycle of deception.

Fabricating lies and creating evidence impose a significant cognitive load and mental effort on the liar. The constant vigilance required to maintain consistency and evade detection can be mentally exhausting. This cognitive strain can impede other cognitive processes and compromise overall cognitive functioning.

Engaging in deception often invites suspicion and scrutiny from others. Once a person's credibility comes into question, their every word and action are subjected to heightened scrutiny. This increased scrutiny can create an atmosphere of suspicion, making it challenging for the liar to navigate social interactions with ease.

Moreover, lies carry legal and ethical risks. Depending on the nature and consequences of the deception, individuals may find themselves entangled in legal disputes or facing severe ethical consequences. The web of lies they weave may eventually ensnare them in a trap of their own making.

Given these potential motives, methods, and outcomes of fabricating lies and creating evidence, it becomes crucial to exercise awareness and critical thinking when encountering and communicating information. By developing a vigilant mind-set, one can navigate the intricate web of deception and strive for a more truthful and authentic existence.

Chapter 27

The task of detecting lies and fabricated evidence is a complex one, as there is no universal cue or fool proof method that guarantees accurate results. However, there are some techniques that may enhance the accuracy of lie detection:

One effective approach is to impose cognitive load on the person suspected of lying. By making the act of lying more mentally demanding, the goal is to place a heavier burden on their cognitive resources. This can be achieved through various means, such as asking them to recall their story in reverse order, multitasking by performing a secondary task while answering questions, or maintaining strong eye contact throughout the interaction. Imposing cognitive load can increase the likelihood of detecting inconsistencies, errors, or signs of nervousness in both their verbal and nonverbal behaviour.

Another useful tactic is to encourage the person to provide more information about their story. Instead of relying on simple yes/no questions that allow for brief and vague responses, open-ended questions that require detailed and expansive answers should be utilized. Truthful individuals tend to provide additional relevant information when prompted, while those who are lying may struggle to fabricate more details or may inadvertently contradict themselves. By extracting more information, the chances of identifying contradictions, implausibility's, or deviations from the norm in their statements are heightened.

Asking unexpected questions that catch the person off guard can also be an effective strategy. These questions should be relevant to their story but not obvious or predictable, catching them by surprise. Truthful individuals are typically able to respond quickly and consistently to unexpected questions, while those who are lying may exhibit hesitation, confusion, or evasion in their attempts to invent new lies or avoid answering altogether. This technique increases the likelihood of uncovering deceptive behaviour.

Despite these methods, it is important to acknowledge that lie detection is not infallible and its effectiveness may vary depending on the situation and the individual involved. Caution and critical thinking should be exercised when evaluating the information and evidence presented by others. It is crucial to consider additional factors that can influence credibility, including the motives, emotions, personality traits, and the relationship between the person and the interviewer.

Assessing credibility goes beyond relying solely on lie detection techniques. It requires a comprehensive evaluation of the context, background information, and the overall behaviour and demeanour of the individual in question. Understanding their motives for lying, their emotional state, and their personality traits can provide valuable insights into their credibility. Furthermore, considering the dynamics of the relationship between the interviewer and the person being assessed can shed light on potential biases or conflicts of interest that may influence the information being presented.

In addition to these factors, it is essential to exercise empathy and cultural sensitivity during the lie detection process. Different individuals may exhibit varying behavioural patterns and cultural norms when communicating, making it crucial to account for these differences when evaluating credibility. By embracing a well-rounded and comprehensive approach to lie detection, we can strive for greater accuracy in assessing the veracity of information and evidence presented to us.

Enhancing your lie detection skills is a valuable endeavour that can greatly impact your ability to engage in honest and authentic interactions with those around you. There are several strategies you can employ to improve your lie detection abilities:

One crucial step is to familiarize yourself with the common verbal and nonverbal cues associated with deception. These cues may include signs of nervousness, uncertainty, inconsistency, evasion, or a lack of detail. However, it's essential to recognize that these cues are not fool proof indicators of deception and can vary depending on the context, individual, and type of lie being told. Rather than relying on a single cue, it's important to look for a combination of cues that may suggest deception.

Developing your observation and intuition skills is another effective method for honing your lie detection abilities. By actively observing people's behaviour and expressions in various situations, such as through movies, TV shows, interviews, or real-life interactions, you can train yourself to recognize subtle cues that may indicate dishonesty. Engaging in activities like muting the sound while watching a film or attempting to decipher the emotions and dialogue solely through body language and facial expressions can also sharpen your observational skills.

Asking open-ended questions is a powerful technique to encourage individuals to provide more information and delve deeper into their stories. Rather than relying on simple yes/no questions, posing queries that necessitate detailed and elaborate responses can shed light on the veracity of their claims. Additionally, requesting the person to repeat their story in reverse order or provide specific evidence or examples to support their statements can increase the cognitive load on someone who is being deceptive, potentially leading them to make mistakes or reveal inconsistencies.

Employing unexpected questions can catch individuals off guard and potentially expose deception. By posing relevant yet unpredictable queries that they haven't anticipated or prepared for, you may elicit hesitation, avoidance, or contradictions in their responses.

Engaging in discussions with others who have also observed the person in question can be advantageous. By exchanging perspectives, comparing observations, and collectively analysing the situation, you can enhance the accuracy of your assessments. Research has demonstrated that group discussions can improve lie detection accuracy compared to individual judgments[6].

It is vital to recognize that these methods are not infallible and may not yield consistent results in every situation or with every person. Therefore, it is imperative to approach the evaluation of information and evidence provided by others with caution and critical thinking. Consider additional factors that may impact credibility, including the individual's motives, emotions, personality traits, and your relationship with them.

Maintaining a healthy scepticism while assessing credibility is essential. Avoid jumping to conclusions based solely on observed behaviours or cues. Instead, consider the broader context and corroborating evidence. Understanding the individual's motivations for deception, their emotional state, and their unique personality traits can provide valuable insights into their credibility.

Furthermore, cultural sensitivity is key when assessing behaviours and cues associated with deception. Different cultural backgrounds may influence communication styles and nonverbal expressions, so it is important to be mindful of these variations and avoid making unfounded assumptions based on cultural differences.

In conclusion, improving your lie detection skills requires a multifaceted approach that combines knowledge of common cues, practiced observation, effective questioning techniques, and the exchange of perspectives with others. It is important to remember that lie detection is not an exact science and should be complemented with critical thinking, contextual analysis, and an understanding of human behaviour. By continuously honing your lie detection skills, you can navigate interactions with greater discernment and authenticity, fostering more genuine and trustworthy relationships.

Chapter 28

Refraining from lying to others can be a formidable yet gratifying endeavour, as it paves the way for trust, integrity, and authenticity to flourish within your relationships. However, achieving this goal requires diligent effort and a commitment to self-improvement. Let us explore some insightful and creative ways through which you can prevent yourself from succumbing to the allure of deception.

First and foremost, embark on a journey of honesty by acknowledging and admitting to yourself that you have a propensity for lying. By facing this truth head-on, you create a foundation for personal growth and transformation. Seek to understand the underlying motives behind your lies, whether they stem from fear, insecurity, guilt, or shame. Engaging in introspection enables you to grasp the emotional drivers behind your deceptive behaviour and lays the groundwork for change. Additionally, reflect upon the consequences and costs incurred by your lies, such as the erosion of respect, credibility, and valuable opportunities. Recognizing the impact of your actions empowers you to make more informed choices.

Hold yourself accountable by sharing your journey with a trusted confidant—a friend, family member, or therapist—who can provide support and guidance. This person can serve as a compassionate sounding board, aiding you in monitoring your progress and celebrating your successes. Establish a goal to speak the truth more consistently each day, rewarding yourself for each instance of honesty and acknowledging the strides you make along the way.

Identify and confront the triggers that propel you toward dishonesty. By recognizing the situations, emotions, or circumstances that often lead you astray, you can better equip yourself to resist the temptation to lie. Prepare genuine and authentic responses in advance for those moments when falsehoods might beckon. Cultivate the strength to say no and establish personal boundaries when you feel pressured or uneasy. Equipping yourself with premeditated honesty empowers you to navigate challenging situations with integrity.

Adopt a new mind-set that treats lying as an addictive behaviour. Embrace the understanding that deceit is not a solution but rather a problem that can inflict harm upon both yourself and others. Challenge the beliefs and rationalizations that have allowed your lies to persist, such as the notion that they are necessary or harmless. By deconstructing these justifications, you pave the way for profound personal growth and liberation from the chains of deception.

Imbue your journey with acceptance and compassion—for both yourself and others. Embrace self-acceptance, free from the need to lie in order to impress or please those around you. Embrace the reality of your circumstances without resorting to falsehoods as an escape or coping mechanism. Furthermore, nurture a compassionate mind-set toward yourself and others, allowing empathy to guide your interactions. Embrace the understanding that lies are not necessary to avoid causing harm or being hurt. By fostering acceptance and compassion, you create a fertile environment for honesty to flourish.

It is vital to acknowledge that these methods are not easily accomplished and may necessitate significant time, effort, and even professional assistance. Therefore, exercise patience and persistence on your journey, recognizing that personal growth is an on-going process. Do not hesitate to seek support when needed, as guidance from trusted individuals or professionals can provide invaluable insights and encouragement. Remember, refraining from lying is not a punishment but rather a gift—a gift you bestow upon yourself and those you care about.

As you embark on this transformative endeavour, embrace the possibilities that await. Embrace the freedom that accompanies living an honest and authentic life. By committing to the path of truth, you forge stronger connections, build trust, and embark on a profound journey of self-discovery and genuine human connection.

Epilogue
Embracing the Truth

As we come to the end of our journey through the intricate web of lies and deception, we find ourselves standing at a crossroads. The knowledge we have acquired throughout this book has opened our eyes to the pervasive nature of deceit, both in ourselves and in the world around us. Now, in this final chapter, we turn our attention to the transformative power of truth and the profound impact it can have on our lives.

Throughout the preceding chapters, we explored the many facets of deception, from its psychological underpinnings to its manifestations in various aspects of human existence. We examined how self-deception shields us from uncomfortable realities and how we employ deceptive tactics to influence others. We scrutinized the ways in which deceit pervades our relationships, our work, and our society at large. But amidst this sea of deception, there is an anchor that holds the potential to set us frees—the truth.

Truth, though often elusive and challenging to uncover, possesses an extraordinary ability to bring about personal growth and forge genuine connections with others. When we embrace the truth, we embark on a path of self-discovery and authenticity. We confront our own biases and acknowledge our flaws, paving the way for personal growth and a more profound understanding of ourselves. The truth becomes a compass that guides us towards our true potential.

Furthermore, embracing the truth enables us to cultivate meaningful connections with those around us. Genuine relationships are built on trust, and trust can only flourish in an environment of honesty and transparency. When we are honest with ourselves and others, we create a space for vulnerability, empathy, and understanding. The walls of deception crumble, making room for genuine human connection and fostering a sense of belonging.

But embracing the truth is not always an easy path to tread. It requires courage and a willingness to confront uncomfortable truths. It necessitates self-reflection and the humility to admit when we are wrong. It demands that we challenge our own preconceived notions and be open to the perspectives of others. Yet, the rewards that await us on this path are immeasurable.

When we embrace the truth, we free ourselves from the burdens of self-deception. We no longer need to maintain a facade or protect our fragile egos. Instead, we can celebrate our authentic selves and find solace in the knowledge that we are living in alignment with our values and beliefs.

Moreover, embracing the truth empowers us to navigate the complexities of a world steeped in deception. Armed with a discerning eye, we can recognize the manipulative tactics employed by others and protect ourselves from their influence. We become critical thinkers, capable of deciphering fact from fiction and making informed decisions based on reliable information.

As we close the final chapter of this book, we invite you, the reader, to embrace the truth in all its forms. Seek truth within yourself, unearthing your authentic desires, values, and aspirations. Embrace the truth in your interactions with others, fostering honesty, empathy, and trust. Hold truth as a guiding principle in your pursuit of knowledge and understanding, and let it illuminate your path.

In doing so, we believe that you will not only transform your own life but also contribute to a world that desperately needs truth and integrity. Each individual who embraces the truth becomes a beacon of light, dispelling the darkness of deception and fostering a society rooted in honesty and authenticity.

So, as we bid farewell to these pages filled with insights and revelations, let us carry the lessons learned with us. Let us embark on a journey of self-discovery, armed with the power of truth. And let us forge a future where the shadows of deception fade and the brilliance of truth guides us toward a brighter tomorrow.

In embracing the truth, we discover our true selves. In embracing the truth, we uncover the path to genuine connection. In embracing the truth, we find liberation from the shackles of deception. May this epilogue serve as a reminder that the pursuit of truth is a lifelong endeavour—one that holds the promise of personal growth, meaningful relationships, and a more enlightened world.

Acknowledgments

Writing a book of this nature is a collaborative effort that involves the support and contribution of many individuals. As we come to the end of this journey, we would like to express our heartfelt gratitude to all those who have played a part in bringing this project to fruition.

First and foremost, we would like to thank our families and loved ones for their unwavering support throughout the process. Their understanding, encouragement, and patience have been instrumental in allowing us to dedicate the time and energy needed to undertake this endeavour.

We extend our deepest appreciation to our editor and the entire publishing team who believed in the value of this book and guided us with their expertise and insights. Their dedication and commitment to excellence have helped shape this work into its final form.

We are indebted to the numerous researchers, psychologists, and experts in the field of deception and human behaviour whose studies and findings have served as the foundation for this book. Their tireless efforts in unravelling the intricacies of deception have paved the way for a deeper understanding of ourselves and the world we inhabit.

We would also like to express our gratitude to the individuals who generously shared their personal stories and experiences with us. Their willingness to open up and discuss the complex nature of deception has added depth and authenticity to our work.

To our friends and colleagues who provided valuable feedback and engaged in thought-provoking discussions, we extend our sincerest thanks. Your input and perspectives have enriched the content of this book and challenged us to delve deeper into the subject matter.

Additionally, we would like to acknowledge the countless readers who have embarked on this journey with us. Your curiosity, engagement, and support have been a constant source of inspiration. It is our hope that the ideas and insights presented in these pages resonate with you and lead to meaningful introspection and discussions.

Lastly, we would like to acknowledge the enduring power of truth. It is a force that transcends boundaries, breaks down barriers, and brings about positive change. The importance of truth in our lives cannot be overstated, and we are humbled by the opportunity to explore its significance through this book.

In conclusion, we extend our deepest gratitude to each and every person who has contributed to the creation of this book. Your support, whether big or small, has been invaluable. May our collective commitment to embracing the truth guide us toward a future that is marked by authenticity, understanding, and genuine human connection.

Thank you.

R.ANANDA RAJU

DISCLAIMER:

The information contained in this book is provided for general informational purposes only. While every effort has been made to ensure the accuracy and completeness of the information presented, the author and the publisher make no representations or warranties of any kind, express or implied, about the completeness, accuracy, reliability, suitability, or availability with respect to the contents of this book. Any reliance you place on such information is therefore strictly at your own risk.

The author and the publisher disclaim any liability for any errors or omissions in the content of this book. They shall not be held responsible or liable for any loss or damage, including but not limited to indirect or consequential loss or damage, arising out of or in connection with the use of this book.

The opinions expressed in this book are solely those of the author and do not necessarily reflect the views of the publisher. The inclusion of any external sources or references does not imply endorsement or validation by the author or the publisher.

Any resemblance to actual persons, living or dead, or actual events is purely coincidental.

By purchasing, reading, or using this book, you acknowledge that you have read and understood this Copyright and Disclaimer Certificate and agree to abide by its terms and conditions.